W9-AFK-882

PRESENTING

Robert Cormier

UPDATED EDITION

TUSAS 496

Twayne's United States Authors Series
Young Adult Authors

The Young Adult Authors books seek to meet the need for critical studies of fiction for young adults. Each volume examines the life and work of one author, helping both teachers and readers of young adult literature to understand better the writers they have read with such pleasure and fascination.

PRESENTING
Robert Cormier

UPDATED EDITION

Patricia J. Campbell

Twayne Publishers • Boston
A Division of G. K. Hall & Co.

Presenting Robert Cormier, Updated Edition
Patricia J. Campbell

Published by Twayne Publishers
A division of G. K. Hall & Co.
70 Lincoln Street
Boston, Massachusetts 02111

Photographs and captions kindly provided by Robert Cormier.

First edition copyright 1985 by G. K. Hall & Co.

Copyediting supervised by Barbara Sutton.
Book production by Janet Z. Reynolds.
Typeset by Crane Typesetting Service, Inc.

Printed on permanent/durable acid-free paper
and bound in the United States of America

Library of Congress Cataloging in Publication Data

Campbell, Patricia J.
Presenting Robert Cormier / Patricia J. Campbell. — Updated ed.
p. cm. — (Twayne's United States authors series ; TUSAS
496. Young adult authors)
Bibliography: p.
Includes index.
ISBN 0-8057-8212-5
1. Cormier, Robert—Criticism and interpretation. 2. Young adult
fiction, American—History and criticism. I. Title. II. Series:
Twayne's United States authors series ; TUSAS 496. III. Series:
Twayne's United States authors series. Young adult authors.
PS3553.0653Z6 1989
813'.54—dc20

89-33707
CIP

For Mel Rosenberg,
who opened the door

LIES

Telling lies to the young is wrong.
Proving to them that lies are true is wrong.
Telling them that God's in his heaven
and all's well with the world is wrong.
The young know what you mean. The young
are people.
Tell them the difficulties can't be counted,
and let them see not only what will be
but see with clarity these present times.
Say obstacles exist they must encounter,
sorrow happens, hardship happens.
The hell with it. Who never knew
the price of happiness will not be happy.
Forgive no error you recognize,
it will repeat itself, increase,
and afterwards our pupils
will not forgive in us what we forgave.

—Yevgeny Yevtushenko

Contents

Acknowledgments

First of all, an immeasurable amount of gratitude is owed to Robert Cormier himself for his enthusiasm and helpfulness in the preparation of this book. I wish to thank both Mr. and Mrs. Cormier and also their daughter Renee for their gracious hospitality during the time I was a guest at their home in Leominster, Massachusetts, in January 1984 and September 1988. During these visits, Mr. Cormier shared his memories, thoughts, ideas, and unpublished manuscripts with unstinting generosity almost nonstop. Throughout this book the sources for any otherwise undocumented facts and quotations are to be found in the notes and tape recordings from these extended interviews.

Hearty thanks are also due to the Robert E. Cormier Collection of the Special Collections Department of the Library of Fitchburg State College, Fitchburg, Massachusetts, and to the expertise and kindness of its curator, Special Collections Librarian Robert Foley, in making the riches of the collection available repeatedly at a moment's notice. No information request was too small or too unusual for his instant energetic and conscientious attention.

Special thanks, too, are owed Emily McKeigue, who conceived and developed the idea for this series, and to Caroline Birdsall for her continuing strong overall editorial support. A very large thank-you goes to Ron Brown, series editor for the first edition, for his lavish encouragement, praise, and hospitality far beyond formal editorial duty. Most of all, I am grateful for the privilege of working closely with the in-house editor for the Young Adult Authors Series, Athenaide Dallett, whose brilliance is tempered with wisdom and tact.

Appreciation is given to Judy Gitenstein, formerly of Avon Books, for copies of the early Cormier novels; to Sherry Gerstein of

Alfred A. Knopf for books and many reviews; to George Nicholson, Suzanne Murphy, and Olga Litowinsky of Delacorte Press for information and galleys, and to Anita Silvey of *Horn Book* for advance proofs of the interview on *Beyond the Chocolate War* and the essay on *Fade*.

The author gratefully acknowledges permission to quote from the following sources: "In Memory of Sigmund Freud" from *W. H. Auden: Collected Poems*, edited by Edward Mendelson, copyright © 1940, 1968, 1979 by W. H. Auden, reprinted by permission of Random House, Inc.; *The Waste Land* in *Collected Poems 1909–1962* by T. S. Eliot, copyright 1936 by Harcourt Brace Jovanovich, Inc., © 1963, 1964 by T. S. Eliot, reprinted by permission of Harcourt Brace Jovanovich, Inc.; and "Lies" from *Selected Poems* by Yevgeny Yevtushenko, trans. Robin Milner-Gulland and Peter Levi (Penguin Modern European Poets 1962), p. 52, © 1962 by Robin Milner-Gulland and Peter Levi, reprinted by permission of Penguin Books Ltd.

Chronology

1925 Robert Edmund Cormier born 17 January in Leominster, Massachusetts.

1943 Enrolls in Fitchburg State College, Fitchburg, Massachusetts.

1944 First published short story, "The Little Things That Count," in the *Sign*.

1946 Begins work for radio station WTAG, Worcester, Massachusetts.

1948 Transferred to night staff of Leominster bureau of *Worcester Telegram and Gazette*. Marries Constance Senay, 6 November.

1951 Daughter Roberta born.

1953 Son Peter born.

1955 Becomes a reporter for *Fitchburg Sentinel*.

1957 Daughter Christine born.

1959 Promoted to wire editor, *Fitchburg Sentinel*. Best human-interest story of the year, Associated Press in New England.

1960 *Now and at the Hour*.

1963 *A Little Raw on Monday Mornings*.

1965 *Take Me Where the Good Times Are*.

1966 Becomes associate editor and columnist, *Fitchburg Sentinel*.

1967 Daughter Renee born.

1973 Best human-interest story of the year, Associated Press in New England.

1974 *The Chocolate War*. Best newspaper column, K. R. Thomson Newspapers.

1977 *I Am the Cheese.*

1977 Honorary doctor of letters, Fitchburg State College.

1979 *After the First Death.*

1980 *Eight Plus One.*

1981 Robert E. Cormier Collection established at Fitchburg State College.

1983 *The Bumblebee Flies Anyway.*

1985 *Beyond the Chocolate War.*

1988 *Fade*

1. Bike Ride in Winter

You are riding the bicycle and you are on Route 2 thirty miles west of Boston on your way to Leominster, Massachusetts, and you're pedaling furiously because this is an old-fashioned bike, no speeds, no fenders, only the warped tires and the brakes that don't always work and the handle-bars with cracked rubber grips to steer with. A plain bike—the kind Bob Cormier rode as a kid years ago. It's cold as you pedal along, the wind like a snake slithering up your sleeves and into your jacket and your pants legs, too. But you keep pedaling, you keep pedaling.

It's crazy to be riding a bicycle here on the snowy highway in the midst of winter. But this is a pilgrimage, a journey to Cormier country, and riding a bike—an *old* bike—is the only right way to do it. This is the kind of bicycle Adam Farmer rode on his perpetual haunted journey to find his dead father, and Cormier's words from the beginning of *I Am the Cheese* echo again in your head as you struggle uphill against the bitter wind. "I am riding the bicycle and I am on Route 31 in Monument, Massachusetts, on my way to Rutterburg, Vermont, and I'm pedaling furiously because this is an old-fashioned bike. . . ."

You look back over your shoulder, but there's no one following.

The low hills are covered with patches of snow, and the naked trees are rows of black pen-scratches slashed between the white ground and the white sky. You labor on, careful to stay in the tracks of clear pavement left by the snow tires of cars. Near the brow of the hill is a sign: "Leominster. The Pioneer Plastic City. Population 38,000." As you come over the crest you see the town straggling across the little valleys below, a jumble of clapboard and dull red brick from the turn of the century. An ugly New England mill town, but with a comfortable air of homeyness and endurance.

Leominster and the neighboring town of Fitchburg are where Robert Cormier has lived all of his life. As Monument, Massachusetts, they are the setting for his stories, the theater where his characters struggle against the ominous powers of malice and tyranny that gather like the dark snowclouds behind these hills of Leominster. The people in his novels are creatures of his own mind, but the stage sets for their grim dramas are the streets and schools and houses of these two tiny towns where Robert Cormier's own life has been acted out. It is to visit these places that you have made this cold, slippery journey—to see these real places in "Monument" where Jerry Renault and Adam Farmer and Amy Hertz and Miro Shantas walked and worried and dreamed, and to see what kind of man could be the creator of these brave and tormented people.

You follow the directional signs off the highway to a smaller road. At the top of the hill you pause to rest, breathing heavily, and to settle the newspaper-wrapped package more securely in your bike basket. It is soggy now from the damp cold air and some of the Scotchtape has begun to pull free. You turn up your jacket collar around your ears, push off, and sail in one long swoop down Main Street through the town and on to the town square, the Common on the north of the center of the business district where Main Street widens out to form a triangle. This is where Jerry Renault waited for the bus, leaning wearily against a telephone pole after a grueling football practice. On the Common by the Civil War cannon and the flagpole the grass has long been covered with snow, and no hippies lounge about or cross the street to challenge Jerry to start his own war, his Chocolate War. A bus pulls up with a hiss and a stench of exhaust.

You cross the square, wheeling the bike through the crosswalks, and look up at the third floor of the rooming house from *Take Me Where the Good Times Are*. Behind these windows Jean Baptiste in his lonely insanity clung to the secret companionship of his family of dolls. Even from where you stand on the sidewalk you can smell the lonesome smell of food fried on a hot plate.

Careful of the traffic now, you pedal slowly down Pleasant Street to Mechanic Street and turn left. A few blocks farther on, you come to the heart of Cormier country, the district called French Hill. This is the neighborhood of Cormier's childhood. Here he grew up in a warm, close community of family and friends, all French Canadian immigrants who had come to New England in the early part of the century to provide manpower for the newly built factories. The narrow clapboard houses stand sturdy and square, three stories with white-trimmed shutters and balconies. Each is set apart on its own bare little plot of land, but no fences separate neighbors and friends. "Tenements" they are called hereabouts, but these decent working-people's homes are nothing like the disreputable tenements of New York City.

You wheel along the quiet streets and stop for a moment in tribute in front of the pale green house where Alph LeBlanc in *Now and at the Hour* fought his silent losing battle with cancer —and where Cormier's own father died in his son's arms. Above the bare branches of the elm trees you can see the spire of St. Cecelia's Church—or St. Jude's Church in Monument. When you come abreast of its facade you glance apprehensively across the street to the third floor balcony—but Paul Moreaux is not to be seen. Around the corner on Sixth Street you pass number 121, where Cormier (and Paul) lived as a little child and where the Midnight Raiders from *Eight Plus One* plotted their vegetable raids. Down the block is the bar called the Happy Times in *A Little Raw on Monday Mornings*, where lonely middle-aged Gracie had her one night of fun, and where Cormier father and son came to watch baseball games together on television. Through the widely spaced houses and tree trunks you can see downhill across Mechanic Street to the factories where Cormier's relatives and his characters Alph and Gracie and Tommie and Louis worked all their lives on the comb machines.

You turn back to town now and, trying to avoid the traffic in the square, you turn left into a narrow alley. A mistake, you soon realize—it goes nowhere. But a voice in your head says, "Lose something, honey?," and you look up to discover Fat Arthur's fire escape. The iron railings and banisters and rungs are cagelike, and you remember that he sat there in the pages of *I Am the Cheese* like a prisoner in his weight and bulk. Hurriedly you back out of the dank alley and steer determinedly up Mechanic Street and then north toward Fitchburg.

Your legs churn with rhythm, tempo, and as you fly along the road you think about the meanings of the word *monument*: A structure erected as a memorial for valiant deeds. A place preserved as having special historical importance. An inscribed stone in remembrance of the dead. An exceptional example of something. From the Latin for "to remind, to warn." One by one you measure them for appropriateness as you bicycle through Monument, Massachusetts.

It's a long way to Fitchburg, and long before you get there your hands are rigid claws around the handlebars. At last you reach the outskirts, and, a minute later, the center of Fitchburg. Although this town is almost the same size as Leominster, Main Street seems more "downtown." You wobble through the stream of cars and trucks and pull up in front of the brick and stone facade of the public library. Should you go in for a minute? It would feel good to get warm, but time is short and you have miles to go before the dark comes. You put one foot out to balance yourself and step deep into a snowbank. The icy prickles down your boot make up your mind for you. You go carefully up the slippery walk and push open the door where Amy and Adam first met. She was coming in and he was going out, you remember, and they collided, spilling books everywhere; before they finished picking them up he was madly in love.

But you're just cold. In the sudden welcome warmth and light you stroll up and down the aisles, rubbing the feeling back into your cold fingers. In the fiction section you find Cormier's three early adult books—*Now and at the Hour, A Little Raw on Monday*

Mornings, and *Take Me Where the Good Times Are*. Where is *Eight Plus One*, you wonder? In the short-story section? Or probably on the Young Adult shelves, along with *The Chocolate War, I Am the Cheese*, and *After the First Death*. The librarian smiles pleasantly at you, and you are tempted to stay to talk with her about your pilgrimage. You have heard that Robert Cormier serves on the board of trustees for the Leominster Public Library. But you glance out the window and see that the late afternoon light is starting to fade.

Hurrying now, you pedal along Main Street a little farther, past the spot where the *Fitchburg Sentinel* offices used to be. A new building stands there now, but you imagine Cormier standing at the window of the office where he worked for so many years as associate editor. At another window Amy's father gazes out, taking a moment's break from his work as editor of the *Monument Times*.

At the intersection of Main and Mechanic streets (a *different* Mechanic Street) you pause at the curb and peer up the street to your right, where the hospital looms on a rise. Adam thinks his father is there sometimes, and Barney could have been there, too, waiting out his short life in The Complex, yearning for the Bumblebee to fly anyway. You think you glimpse a high fence, too, that could hide an automobile graveyard.

After a minute you make a U-turn and start back south toward Leominster. Several miles off to the west you know is the sinister presence of Fort Devens—or Fort Delta. There too are the culvert and the high railroad bridge where the terrorists held Kate and the children prisoner in the school bus. Two separate places, actually, although Cormier put *this* bridge across *that* culvert in his mind and in his book to make the set for *After the First Death*. You would like to visit these places, but they are miles away, and besides, they wouldn't let you into Fort Delta, you tell yourself.

One more stop left, now, an important one, and then on to the final destination. At the thought of what lies at the end of your journey a shiver of anticipation—or is it dread?—travels through your stomach. You pedal faster and try to block out your thoughts by concentrating on the pain in your calves. Tempo, rhythm. . . . Your feet rise and fall, around and around. Overhead the street lights begin to wink on.

Breathing hard, you pass Notre Dame Preparatory School, where Cormier's son Peter, with his father's approval, refused to sell chocolates. This is Trinity School, where Jerry Renault dared disturb the universe, and up ahead is your last stop, the athletic field. You take a small side road that brings you around and above. You lean your bike against a tree and pick your way through the little wood until you can see down the slope to where a few players are finishing a late football practice under stadium lights. The paint on the shabby bleachers on the far side of the field is sickly green under the illumination. The ground has been cleared of snow, but the muddy puddles near the goal posts are frozen slick. The cries and thuds of the practice are like the brutal fight sounds that Brother Leon heard as he stood hidden and gloating here among these trees. Now the tired players are leaving the field with their helmets under their arms. Suddenly the lights are switched off and the dark falls over your head like a blanket. Your ears ring with an animal roar from the empty grandstand. The night has come on while you have been standing here.

In the darkness. You blunder back through the trees, stumbling over rocks, and grab your bike with stiff hands. Your ears sing with pain from the bitter cold as your legs churn urgently toward the final destination. Not too far, now, not too far. But what will you find at the end? Because the object of your pilgrimage is, of course, Robert Cormier himself. What kind of man could have written these books that show so clearly the face of evil? What kind of man can look so deeply into the heart of darkness?

The houses are far back from the road now as you sail past, and a line from *Take Me Where the Good Times Are* sneaks into your mind: "There's a dark and lonesome spot in every town where the bright, shining stores come to an end and the buildings rise out of the darkness, the pale street lights flickering in the tree branches like candles for the dead." Almost there, almost there, you tell yourself. Then you hear a faint rhythmic clinking of a bicycle chain making a duet with your own. Close behind a swishing of tires. Someone else crazy enough to ride a bike in this terrible dark cold? You hesitate in surprise to listen, and he sweeps past, bent over his handlebars, doggedly pedaling on and on, through his fantasies and through his fears—Adam in his father's old jacket with his knit cap pulled down over his ears. Up ahead he fades into the blackness and somewhere you hear a dog barking a bark with a snarl in it.

Your front wheel swoops wildly. You fight for control and narrowly miss falling into the snow that gleams dully from the side of the road. But there it is, two doors farther on, the Cormier house, tucked under tall black pines like the witch's cottage in the woods. What will you find when you knock on the door? It doesn't matter; you are desperate for light and warmth.

You wheel your tired old bike up the driveway and lay it against the front porch. You take your package out of the basket, the package that holds your well-thumbed copies of *Chocolate War* and *I Am the Cheese*. Was it childish to have brought them for Cormier to autograph, you wonder fleetingly?

But then you are at the door knocking, and it opens immediately. A slight man with wispy gray hair and a crooked smile like sunshine holds out his hand. Behind him you see a handsome motherly woman and a pretty dark-haired girl. "Come in, come in," he cries in a voice full of welcome and concern. "We've been worried about you! You must be just frozen! Connie's made some hot chocolate for you—come in!" And you step out of the dark into a house full of comfort and warmth.

2. The Monster as Clark Kent

The man who has just opened the door is Robert Cormier. This is the writer who has been called one of the finest unsung novelists in America today.[1] The *New York Times Book Review* described him, quite accurately, as "the picture of a small-city newspaperman—slight, sort of wispy, gray; a man who's reported the fires and Lions Club meetings and courthouse corruption. He's also a nice man, a family man. . . ."[2] They forgot to say that his eyes gaze straight at you with kindly frankness from behind his big glasses and that his ears are endearingly large. He doesn't look like a man who writes novels of stunning impact about the monstrous and inexorable power of evil. He looks like Clark Kent.

He himself recognizes the paradox. He has written: "Look at me: I cry at sad novels, long for happy endings, delight in atrocious puns, pause to gather branches of bittersweet at the side of a highway. I am shamelessly sentimental—I always make a wish when I blow out the candles on my birthday cake, and I dread the day when there may be no one there to say 'Bless you' when I sneeze. . . . I hesitate to kill a fly, but people die horrible deaths in my novels."[3] "These are terrifying times," he muses. "I'm terrified half the time. The strange thing is, basically I'm an optimistic person."

His sunny compassion shows up in innumerable small ways. If you ask how to pronounce his name (Is it Cor-MEER? Cor-mee-

AY?) he will assure you that the version you have just used is fine, and the way most people say it. But overheard speaking unaware on the phone, he introduces himself as Bob COR-mee-ehr. About to visit a junior high school class, he was warned by the teacher in the hall that the students had been very impressed by the dark aspects of his books and were expecting some sort of monster to walk through the door. So he deliberately tripped as he crossed the threshold, to make himself look silly and to disarm their fears.[4]

Cormier has confessed that Adam Farmer in *I Am the Cheese* is a character that comes close to being autobiographical, not in the events of the story but in the fears and phobias that torment him. Like Adam, Cormier suffers from migraines. "The old drill right here," he says, pointing to his temple. Also like Adam, he is afraid of dogs. "When I was a kid I was chased by a thousand dogs on my paper route. I'm still not that comfortable with them, big ones especially and small ones on certain occasions."[5]

"I am afraid of a thousand things, a million," says Adam. "I mean, elevators panic me. I stand in the upright coffin and my body oozes sweat and my heart pounds and this terrible feeling of suffocation threatens me and I wonder if the doors will ever open." Cormier agrees. For many years a hotel room on the ground floor would have to be found for him when he went on speaking tours, and he and his host would have to climb flights and flights of back stairs to reach auditoriums and receptions. Recently he has worked to overcome this phobia, because, characteristically, he didn't want to continue to put other people to so much trouble. He read up on the mechanisms, talked to elevator operators, and found out that passengers are not really as isolated as it seems, because they can escape through emergency exits if necessary. His fears faded. He is still not entirely comfortable about it, but not long ago he made a triumphant trip up the Sears Tower—seventy-six floors and then an express to the top.

The daily events of his life are peaceful. For twenty-three years he has lived in the same two-story shingled house in a pleasant wooded suburb of Leominster. Here he and his wife, Connie, have raised four children. All are now married and live not too far away. His modest beige Volvo sedan stands in the driveway. The living room has big soft chairs, a snug window seat, a baby grand piano that was given years ago to Connie's mother by her father (a spectacular gift in the depression and an incident that Cormier has used in at least two stories). Several shelves hold tokens and mementos from fans, in the shape of ceramic beehives or plastic school buses or homemade miniature bicycles.

At one end of the dining room is a small alcove that is Cormier's study—the magic phonebooth where Clark Kent rips off his jacket to become Superman. Among the clutter of books and papers is a stereo console, and near the desk is his battered standard reporter's manual Royal typewriter. (At one point he had traded it in for a new electric, but in a few days he went back and retrieved his old friend at a financial loss—much to the shopkeeper's bafflement.) Here in this office without a door Cormier "weaves his writing into the fabric of his existence," as he has said, always available to his family. His years as a newsman have made him immune to noise and distraction when he works.

Cormier often works here late at night. He says, "My daughter Bobbie recently told friends that, for as far back as she can remember, she could hear the tap, tap, tap of typewriter keys as she went off to sleep. She said it was a comforting sound."[6] His insomnia has been a factor in the extraordinary closeness he has had with his own children as they were growing through the teen years. "I'd be awake when my kids came home at night. They knew I wasn't spying on them and we'd just talk. There are a lot of things a kid will tell you at one in the morning that he won't at one in the afternoon. I found their lives exciting and tragic. A kid could go through a whole lifetime in an afternoon on the beach."[7]

All the Cormier teenagers are grown up now and some have children of their own. Renee, the last to emerge from adolescence, is now twenty-one and has just left home to finish her studies in social work at Regis College and to marry a boy she met as a camp counselor two summers ago. Roberta, thirty-seven, was formerly art director for a small publisher, and she and her husband have an adopted daughter, Jennifer. Peter, thirty-five, has a substantial job in insurance and three children—Travis, Darren, and Mallory. Christine, thirty-one, is also married with one daughter, Emily, and has put her master's degree in criminal justice to work in her job as a research associate for a social sciences research firm. All are frequent and welcome visitors at their parents' home.

Cormier's rapport with his own and other young adults has made him extremely open and available to his readers. In *Catcher in the Rye*, Holden Caulfield says, after finishing Isak Dinesen's *Out of Africa*, "What really knocks me out is a book that, when you're all done reading it, you wish the author that wrote it was a terrific friend of yours and you could call him up on the phone whenever you felt like it."[8] Cormier is that kind of author. Teenagers *can* just call him up anytime: it is a well-known secret that Amy Hertz's phone number in *I Am the Cheese* is Cormier's own. His readers do call, often. Sometimes, if they are especially sharp, they ask for Amy. "Sorry, she's not home, but this is her father," says Cormier, or if Renee is visiting and has answered the phone she responds, "Speaking—." Some callers are so shocked by this collision of reality and fantasy that they hang up, but those who persist find Cormier willing to discuss their questions about the books with seriousness and respect. The only time his patience wears thin is when young callers forget time-zone differences and ring the Cormier phone very late at night. "Do you know what *time* it is?" he growls, like everybody's father.

Letters pour in, too, from readers who want to find out why a certain character did what, or the meaning of a puzzling turn in the plot. Typically, boys ask about *The Chocolate War* and girls have questions about *I Am the Cheese*, although there are exceptions. The intricate last chapter of *I Am the Cheese* has drawn so many questions that a class at Fitchburg State College has prepared an answer sheet for Cormier to mail out, revealing the enlightening nuggets of plot facts that can be ferreted out of earlier chapters. But usually he feels that a thoughtful question deserves a personal answer, sometimes as long as two closely written sheets. It distresses him when he finds that a correspondent has forgotten to include a return address, or worse, has written it only on the envelope—which Cormier has already

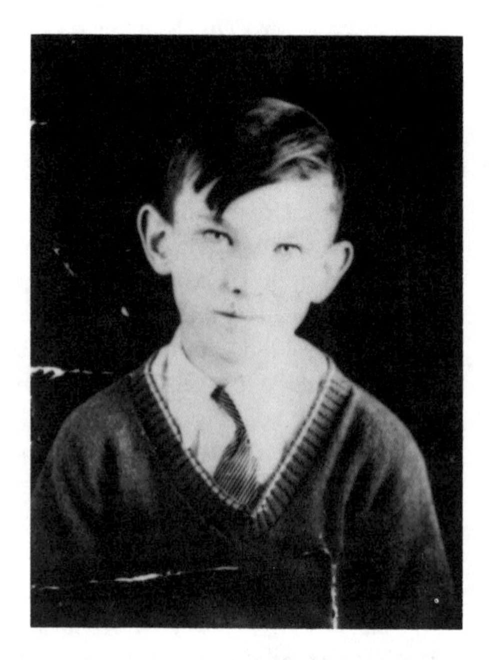

Robert Cormier as a child. "One of those school pictures taken without any warning and with no one to tell you to comb your hair or straighten your tie. Yet, this is me, all right although sometimes I wonder who that boy really is or maybe who I am."

On the shores of Lake Pond, about 1935. From left: Robert, Norman, Irma Cormier holding Gloria.

Lucien Cormier and his children during World War II. Counter-clockwise: Connie, Jack, Robert, Anne, Charlie (Gloria not shown).

Robert and Connie Cormier before their marriage, 1947.

The Cormiers with agent Marilyn Marlow.

The Cormier family after the world premiere of the film of *I Am the Cheese*, 1983. Clockwise: Connie Cormier, Terry (Peter's wife), Lindsay (Chris's husband), Renee, Bobbie, Irma Cormier, Chris, David (Bobbie's husband), Peter, and Robert Cormier.

thrown away. He values the discipline of this feedback from his audience highly: "They keep me sharp. They ask some very tough questions about things I haven't really thought through."

Cormier's willingness to think things through, to face up to the absolute truth without cynicism or bitterness—these qualities give his work strength and integrity. Some of that courage may come from the solidity of a childhood in the secure, self-enclosed community of French Hill, and from the safety of a good marriage and a lifetime in the same town. "I love it here," he says. "I like being able to go downtown and run into some guy I was in the first grade with."[9]

Although Leominster was founded in 1740, the French Hill section was built during the years 1900 to 1915 to house the labor being recruited from Canada for the new comb factories. The French were not the only immigrants—Italians and Irish also poured into the town during this period—but members of each ethnic group kept to their own section. Here Robert Cormier's grandfather brought his young family to America to seek his fortune, and was soon a man of substance with a three-story tenement house and a horse and wagon of his own. His son Lucien Joseph Cormier married an Irish girl, Irma Collins,[10] and brought her back home to live in the ground floor of the tenement his father owned in French Hill.

The first of their eight children, Norman, arrived soon, and two years later, on 17 January 1925, Robert Edmund Cormier was born.[11] With grandparents upstairs and aunts and uncles as neighbors, he was surrounded with love and attention as a small child, although his earliest memory is a sad one. When Robert was five his three-year-old brother Leo died. "My mother said that he was a blond, beautiful child," he remembers. "I was sort of his protector because we were close in age." The family mourned the loss, but other siblings filled the gap: Gloria, John, Anne, and later, when Robert was fourteen, the twins Constance and Charles.

Life in French Hill was good for young Bob, and he has evoked this time and place lovingly in his most autobiographical novel, *Fade*, and in his short stories. "There was a great sense of family.

I always felt as if my father would take care of us." He played in the yard of St. Cecilia's Parochial School with his brothers and sisters and cousins, or watched the men pitch horseshoes after work. The games of the factory baseball clubs were major social occasions. Everyone would come to cheer for fathers or uncles, and afterward the men and older boys would go off to celebrate the victory with a few beers.

The growing Cormier family moved several times, but always within French Hill. "Moving day was a great time. My grandfather would buy a keg of beer and all the neighbors would pitch in. Those big upright pianos they had in those days—they'd struggle up the stairs with them, or on a pulley, and all the kids would hang around to watch. It was a great time."

Local businesses catered to the needs of the French Hill population: Sauve's Market, Nimee's Department Store, Aubuchon Hardware, Vallee's Dairy. . . . Nobody had a telephone, because there was no need. Best friends lived next door or across the street. It was easier just to open the window and call. Nor did anybody need a car, because all the working adults walked the few blocks to the comb factories, which by now had diversified to other plastic objects, baby carriages, and even, for a time, Arrow Shirts.

Because young Bob's mother was Irish, the Cormiers spoke English at home. The nuns at St. Cecilia's Parochial Grammar School taught in both languages: English in the morning and French in the afternoon. At school life was not so easy anymore. "I wasn't athletic. I was a lousy ballplayer who would rather be off reading a book someplace," he recalls.[12] "On the streets I was alone." But there was always the secure retreat of home. It wasn't all bad. "I had a horrible time in parochial school and I also had a great time," he admits.[13] But in another context he has spoken revealingly of "the hell I went through with nuns."

St. Cecilia's School is part of the church that the rest of Leominster calls "the French Cathedral." The tall spire is the central landmark of French Hill. St. Cecilia's size and beauty is an amazing achievement for such a tiny community. Built in 1934 in the midst of the depression, it was considered an Act of Faith by the factory workers, who scraped together their pennies to erect an extravagant house of God. Its soaring white interior is full of light and is almost Calvinistic in its restraint and lack of superfluous decoration. One truly fine piece of sculpture—a graceful reclining statue of the martyred Saint Cecilia—adorns the chancel. The congregation ran out of money before they could buy proper stained glass, so in Bob's childhood the light streamed in through crinkled orange-gold windows. It was like being inside the sun, he thought often with awe.

But some experiences in the church were more awful than awesome. Every Friday afternoon the nuns brought each class in turn to the sanctuary to make confession in preparation for Sunday mass. The confessionals were simple curtained alcoves at one side of the nave. Conveniently nearby, the class was seated in a long row in a pew, while one by one they went up to sit on a little stool in front of the curtain to confess. But the priest inside was deaf. "Louder! Louder!" he'd demand. If you held anything back you'd be unclean for communion, the nuns had told them, and then you'd go straight to hell. So, stiff with agonized embarrassment, Bob would shout out all his small shameful secrets to the avid ears of the row of eavesdroppers behind him.

Other nuns were more sensitive to the budding talent of young Cormier. One especially, Sister Catherine, he remembers with affection as a "big boy's nun." One day, when he was in seventh grade, he sat under the playground stairs and wrote a poem for her. When he handed it to her with trepidation, she read it carefully and said, "Why, Bob! You are a writer!" A casual kindness, but a remark that deeply influenced his self-definition. "Are," not "will be"! From that moment on, he thought of himself as a writer.

These aspirations were refined and shaped by a momentous gift on his twelfth birthday. His Aunt Victorine presented him with *The Adventures of Tom Sawyer*—the first real book he had ever owned. He laughed and cried with Tom, dreamed and schemed with him. "More than that," Cormier wrote in an essay on his childhood reading, "this novel pointed out the drama possible in the life of an ordinary boy and thus the potential drama in my own life. I looked at French Hill as if for the first time and saw its mysteries and its beauties and the drama that can be found in ordinariness."[14]

Although he had always been in love with words, in earlier years young Bob had not been a devotee of the children's room of the Leominster Public Library. "I never found what I was looking for in that children's section because, I see now, I didn't know what I was looking for. . . . I searched in vain for books that would satisfy a yearning in me that I could not identify."[15]

Instead, he pored over comic books—Superman and Terry and the Pirates and the Green Hornet—and devoured the short stories in magazines like *Argosy*, *Liberty*, *Colliers*, and the *Saturday Evening Post*. He came late to books, but after *Tom Sawyer* he persuaded Miss Wheeler, the librarian, to issue him an adult card and began to find in the stacks those authors, such as William Saroyan and Thomas Wolfe, who were to influence his ideas and his adult style.[16]

And then something else happened when he was just about to graduate from eighth grade that marked the end of his accepting childhood and the beginning of his rebelling and questioning adolescence. On the morning of 10 June 1939 he looked up from his school desk and glanced out the window, and there, across the street and beyond a vacant lot, his house was one solid sheet of flame. His mother and baby sister were home, he knew. He leaped to his feet in horror to run, but the teacher, a little bit of a nun who was a ferocious tyrant, cried "Wait! Bob, sit down! We're going to have some prayers before you run out!" And then while the flames crackled she forced him to take out his rosary and say a Decade: an Our Father, ten Hail Marys, and a Glory Be to the Father. When he finally was allowed to leave, he found to his relief that his mother and sister were safe, but the anger from the incident was a force in his life for many years. Much, much later he came to terms with it and was able to forgive and even laugh a little. "They must have been mechanical prayers," he says ruefully.

Although his precious graduation suit had been ruined by the fire, the neighbors rallied round and brought clothes for the Cormiers and he was able to leave St. Cecilia's in dignity. The Leominster public junior high school was another matter. For the first time in his life, he was thrown in with people from a variety of ethnic and religious backgrounds. The French and Italian Catholics entered junior high with a distinct disadvantage: not only were they an exotic minority by religion and national origin, but since their parochial school went on through eighth grade, and public junior high began with seventh grade, they entered an already established social order as outsiders. It was tough.

But there were compensations in his intellectual life. He discovered Saroyan, who had written so movingly of his California Armenian childhood in a community not unlike French Hill. And in ninth grade at the library he found Wolfe, a writer who was to influence him all his life. "His prose thundered like mountain torrents. I simply plunged into his work, somewhere in the middle, reveling in the marvelous tumult of language, getting to know the characters, working back and forth through the chapters."[17] He adored the movies, too, and went faithfully to the Saturday-afternoon matinees in the Plymouth and Met theaters. If he liked the movie, during the week he'd stop by the theater after school and put his ear to the glass door and listen to the dialogue.[18] Because his mother had given up motion pictures as part of a religious vow, young Bob would often hurry home and tell her the week's movie scene by scene—an exercise that taught him the mechanics of plot structure. He kept on writing poetry, too, and some of it was good enough to be published in the *Leominster Daily Enterprise*, much to the pride of French Hill.

In high school his world widened further. For the first time he met a Jew, a girl. In a series of long, intense conversations they told each other everything they knew about their respective religions. More teachers recognized his writing as something special. Several encouraged him. He especially remembers Lillian Ricker, who worked with him, edited his writing, and induced him to start acting. Much to his surprise, he found he was good at it. When the school put on a production of *The Devil and Daniel Webster* he played the second title role with flamboyance and style, and won a "best acting award" for his performance.[19] In spite of his triumphs, he seemed to himself to be a social disaster, particularly with girls. He remembers adolescence as "a lacerating experience." But there was always comfort at home—"once I got in the house I was safe."

World War II was raging when he graduated in 1942. Most of his male classmates were snapped up by the army, but Bob was rejected because of his nearsightedness.[20] He went to work at the factory, as all French Hill sons were expected to do, but he took a night shift so he could go to classes during the day at Fitchburg Teachers College.[21] One of his instructors, Florence Conlon, noticed his skill with words and asked to see something he had written. He showed her a short story, "The Little Things That Count." A few weeks later on a summer Saturday afternoon she drove up in front of the Cormier house, got out of the car, and ran up the walk waving a check. She had had the story typed and had sent it to the *Sign*, a Catholic family magazine. They had accepted it immediately and had sent a check for $75, the first money Cormier had ever earned for his writing.

Encouraged in his ambition to earn his living at the typewriter and eager to get on with it, he left Fitchburg State and took a job writing radio commercials for radio station WTAG. It was excellent discipline for a new writer. Everything had to be packed into a hundred words, and sponsors were severe critics.[22] In the station breaks he was limited to thirty words, and that was even harder.

Independent young bachelors were popular in French Hill. Every Saturday night there were community dances, and Bob loved to dance. First dance would always go to his sister Gloria, and then he would partner each of her girlfriends in turn, spreading his favors around out of courtesy. One Saturday night Gloria arrived with her friend Constance Senay. Connie had been only a sophomore when Bob was a senior at Leominster High. He had been aware of her, but had never really paid any attention to the pretty French Hill girl whose mother ran the pharmacy. But politely he invited her to dance, and they stepped onto the floor together. Forty-two years later he still gets starry-eyed when he describes the next moment. "She was fantastic! We just floated away!" They danced the next dance, and the next, and then there were a succession of Saturday nights, and then they were going together.

Soon he was offered his first real newspaper job. He joined the night staff of the Leominster bureau of the *Worcester Telegram and Gazette* [23] (the paper that owned radio station WTAG). On the strength of the new job he and Connie were married in 1948 at St. Cecilia's Church. The marriage was solid and strong from the very beginning. Connie provided the safe home that gave Cormier a firm foundation for his writing, and her quick intelligence was a match for his brilliance. "The great thing about my wife, Connie, is she has been able to create an atmosphere in which I could work," he was to say many years later.[24] And more. In a short story titled "Another of Mike's Girls" he puts a tribute to Connie into the words of one of his characters: "We have been married twenty-one years and she still has the ability to turn my knees liquid when she holds her head a certain way and looks at me."[25]

In 1955, with two babies at home, he transferred to the competition, the *Fitchburg Sentinel*. He was to work there for the next twenty-three years, first as a reporter; then as wire editor, from 1959 to 1966; and finally as an associate editor and columnist until he left to write full-time in 1978.[26]

From the beginning Cormier was in love with his typewriter. He literally wrote night and day. In the evenings, after a full stint at the newspaper, he did publicity releases for two Fitchburg paper companies to help feed his growing family. Then on the weekends he dove into fiction. "That was my dessert. I wrote stories the way other guys play golf."[27] The *Sign* printed more of his work, and later he became a regular contributor to *Redbook, Woman's Day, McCall's*, the *Saturday Evening Post*, and other popular magazines. His stories were gentle and warm, a little sad, sometimes almost sentimental. He wrote about the small happinesses and disappointments of human relationships, often drawing on his French Hill childhood and adolescence for characters and settings.

This family history material soon grew into a novel, a story of French-Canadian emigrant life told from the point of view of his own grandfather. Although he was not satisfied with the book, he titled it *Act of Contrition* and sent it off in an experimental sort of way to Houghton Mifflin. They rejected it, not to his surprise, but editor Ann Barret was impressed enough to recommend that he find himself an agent. She referred him to the Curtis Brown Agency, where he was taken on by a capable young newcomer from the Midwest, Marilyn Marlow. She encouraged him to continue to explore the novel form in the scarce moments of free time left after his journalistic workday.

Cormier was a very good newspaperman, especially when the assignment had an element of human interest. He won three major journalism awards for his work. In 1959 a piece about a burned child in a car accident earned him the Associated Press award for the best New England news story of the year. In 1973 he was again awarded the same prize for an article about a workshop staffed by mentally retarded people, which was written from their perspective. And in 1974 his human-interest column was judged best in the Thomson Newspaper chain, the syndicate that owned the *Fitchburg Sentinel*.[28]

When the children were young, the Cormiers lived a short way out of town on Pleasant Street in a house with a dormer window that gave a view of the town and the woods. Roberta and Peter rode a bus to a private parochial school in Fitchburg. For a time their parents had considered sending them to public school. Cormier was anxious that his children not suffer under the harsh authority of the nuns as he had done. But in the end they chose a private parochial school, feeling that there, unlike the parish school, the situation would be parent-dominated. In 1959 Cormier even served as PTA president.[29]

Life was good, pleasant, ordinary. And then suddenly the world, like an elevator with a broken cable, dropped from beneath his feet. His father, the strong refuge of his childhood and the closest friend of his adult years, developed lung cancer. Cormier's memories of the progress of his illness are etched deep with the acid of pain.

"I remember the most terrible day of my life. My father had been coughing and losing weight. He went to the doctor to find what the trouble was. As soon as he left the office the doctor called my mother and said, 'The x-ray has revealed a growth, quite large.' So my mother called me and I came down. My father's car pulled up, and through the front window we saw him get out. This endearing typical way he had of tucking up his chest and buttoning his coat with one hand whenever he left the house or got out of a car—he did that, and I thought, '*He does not know*. We know and he doesn't know, and his life is going to change.' He looked so innocent, and it broke my heart.

"The doctor told him he had to have an operation or he would be dead in six months. He had the operation, but he was dead in six months anyway. When he first came home from the hospital he had great hopes. He knew he had to retire, but he had just bought his first car and was looking forward—and then suddenly the pain began."

No one spoke of death. "The doctor had told us, 'See what he says and then follow his lead.' So we did. He never mentioned it, and we never did. People would come to visit him and he just wouldn't speak. We pretended to the end."

Cormier recalls the emotions of that time as anger more than sadness. He began to write about it: "I've always gone to my writing when anything happened to me. It was a natural response." There on the page he spilled out his rage, his loss, his bewilderment over his father's silence. "I wanted to put the whole world in bed with my father and—in a sense—kill them. I just wanted people to know that this man lived and died." So he put himself—and the world—into his dying father's mind, banging away at the typewriter hysterically.

At first it was only therapy, an attempt to rid himself of the anger and shock. But gradually a structure began to emerge. One day his agent, Marilyn Marlow, called to find out why she hadn't gotten any stories from him lately. "Well, I haven't done much writing," he said, "because I've been putting down my thoughts about my father's death."

"I'd like to read it," she said. "I think everything a writer writes is important." He sent her the haphazard heap of paper. She read it through, and called him back. "You know, Bob," she pondered, "with a very little form and work I think this would make a novel that would really affect people."

By this time he had worked off the raw edge of his grief, and had begun to gain insight into his father's death and into the nature of death itself. He saw that she was right. Starting again, he rewrote with an objectivity that had been missing before.

The result was, and was not, autobiographical. Alph LeBlanc in *Now and at the Hour* is not Lucien Cormier. The story, as Cormier later summarized it, tells "how an ordinary man learns of his approaching death, gathers himself to meet it, learns to endure, reaches for shreds of comfort and finally achieves a kind of triumph, lonely though it may be."[30] In the darkness of his grief Cormier had found the theme that was to move through all his novels: the nonhero who struggles to hang on to humanness even under siege from an all-powerful Them—or It.

The book was published almost immediately, and critics, including those at the *Atlantic Monthly*[31] and *Time* magazine,[32] were stunned by its power and honesty and praised it lavishly. The sale was small, less than 5,000 copies, but the word was out that Cormier was a first novelist to watch.

Soon a publisher who had heard of his small-town background approached him with a proposition: a big French Hill epic, a three-generation story about a family from Canada. Initially intrigued by the idea, he struggled with it for six months, recycling the title "Act of Contrition" and using some material from the earlier work. But it was not a congenial task, and eventually he gave it up in disgust. "It was just hack work with no emotion involved," he said later. To Marlow he confided, "I work best with a microscope, not a telescope."[33]

Cormier needed to build a novel from a deeply felt emotion, not just a marketable idea. In a few months that emotion came along. He was sent on assignment to do a story about a woman whose young daughter had been murdered. The assignment included the touchy task of asking the mother for a photograph of the dead child. He sat in the woman's living room and talked with her, established rapport, and got his picture. Later he found his compassion drew him back for another interview and a human-interest story about the woman's tragedy.[34] But he couldn't stop thinking about it. What if, he wondered, this woman were widowed by her husband's reaction to the tragedy? And what if she reached out for just a little comfort—and got pregnant? The "what if" led to a second novel—*A Little Raw on Monday Mornings*, in 1963.

Two years later he wrote another novel that had its genesis in a newspaper assignment. This one came from a visit to an old people's home on the edge of Leominster. Some of the inhabitants impressed him with their spunk. What if—a feisty old man ran away from the home? The comic novel *Take Me Where the Good Times Are* was the answer. The reviews of both books were favorable, but Cormier was beginning to be misunderstood and typecast as a writer who glorified "faceless little people." *Now and at the Hour* cast a giant shadow, and although they were fine in their own way, neither of the next two books measured up to its dark promise.

In 1966, with the pressures of an expanding family, he left newspaper work for a year to experiment with freelancing. He took nonfiction assignments from the magazines that had learned to respect his writing through his short stories. A friend was setting up a new radio station and asked him as a favor to take on the public-relations writing for it. But the hustle of the freelancer's life left him no energy for fiction, and besides, he missed the smell of printer's ink. Back at the newspaper, he threw himself into short-story writing at night. Magazines like *Redbook* were paying as much as $1,500 for a story, and he could turn one out in two weeks. And he continued to write novels and to learn and grow from their creation, although no book he wrote in this period reached publication.

In the mid-1960s his newspaper work and freelance assignments had brought him continually in touch with the racial turmoil that was sweeping the country. "What if it happened in Leominster?" he asked himself. And so a story began to take shape, about a man who wakes up in the hospital terribly burned. He has amnesia from the shock of the accident, but fragments of his past drift into his mind. As he tries to piece together his identity, the doctors are gradually, over a period of days, removing the bandages, and eventually he discovers what everyone else around him has known—he is black. Then there is a mysterious blonde woman, a chase, a sniper in Boston—but history was happening too fast. The novel was hopelessly outdated almost as soon as it was finished, and so "The Rumple Country" was never published. In its theme of amnesia and gradual disclosure of identity, however, it foreshadows more mature treatments of these ideas in *I Am the Cheese* and *The Bumblebee Flies Anyway*.

For the next year and a half he plunged into a book that was his favorite of any he had written up to that time. "In the Midst of Winter" was important to him, both in terms of his personal and spiritual development and in terms of his development as a writer. The title is from Camus: "In the midst of winter, I found that there was in me an invincible summer." It is the story of a worldly young girl, Lily, who is suddenly called to become a nun. Her father is baffled and troubled by her choice, and only years later, after her death, is he inexorably brought to his knees before God. The Hound of Heaven theme (the idea, originated by the poet Francis Thompson, of a lifelong, futile flight from God) fascinated Cormier at this time in his life. Vatican II had brought sweeping changes to the Catholic church, and his own faith was undergoing a revitalization. The book was a vehicle for him to explore the meaning of this spiritual renewal. The character of Lily, too, is significant because she is an early version of the troublesome figure of Cassie, who in first drafts was the protagonist of *The Bumblebee Flies Anyway*. "In the Midst of Winter" was a failure in that it was too intensely Catholic for general publication, but for its author it was a success because of the pleasure and growth he had in the writing of it.

These were his children's teen years. He has described that time vividly in *Eight Plus One*: "The house sang those days with the vibrant songs of youth—tender, hectic, tragic, and ecstatic. Hearts were broken on Sunday afternoon and repaired by the following Thursday evening, but how desperate it all was in the interim. The telephone never stopped ringing, the shower seemed to be constantly running, the Beatles became a presence in our lives."[35]

One day Peter came home from Notre Dame Preparatory with two big shopping bags of chocolates to sell to raise money for the school. At the dinner table that night the family kidded him a bit, then his father came up with three alternatives. Cormier reconstructs the conversation: "I told him, 'Look, Peter, let's just look at the options. First of all, let's have you sell the chocolates. I sold them when I was a kid, and it didn't hurt. You can bother the neighbors and the relatives, and that's all right. Then the second thing would be that we could buy the chocolates.' (Twenty-five boxes, a dollar apiece—I was hoping he wouldn't say yes.) Then the third thing, I said, was 'You know, you don't have to sell the chocolates. It's a free society. It's not going to appear on your report card: CHOCOLATE SALE—FAILURE.' And Peter being who he was, said, 'That sounds fine, Dad. I don't want to sell the chocolates.' So I wrote him a note, and the next day I drove him to school, and as I watched him go up the walk, I thought, 'My God, what am I letting him in for?' "[36] It was September, Peter was a freshman in a very jock school—but nothing happened. He gave the headmaster the letter and the chocolates and that was that.

But something had happened to Cormier. His "what if" had started again. What if the headmaster had been unscrupulous? What if there had been peer pressure? The characters started to come alive, and he began to write *The Chocolate War*. When Marilyn Marlow saw the first chapters she said, "Bob, I think what you have here is a young adult novel." Cormier was alarmed. Would he have to go back and simplify and take things out and clean up the language? Marlow reassured him. "Don't worry about it. Just go on writing what you think is true to what you want to do, and let us determine the market."[37] But some publishers were not as convinced as she that the book was suitable for young people. They found it too downbeat and pressured Cormier to change the ending. He resisted firmly, and eventually Pantheon recognized its quality and put it into print in April 1974 with only minor copyediting.

It was an instant sensation.

Reviewers roared—some in pleasure, some in rage. Controversy developed, but the book's reputation only increased from the tangles with would-be censors. Cormier had found his theme, his tone, his audience.

Two other dark novels of dazzling complexity followed: *I Am the Cheese* in 1977 and *After the First Death* in 1979. Then an intermission in 1980 in the shape of the short-story collection *Eight Plus One*, and in 1983 the strange puzzle of *The Bumblebee Flies Anyway*. Finally, in 1985 his work came full circle with *Beyond the Chocolate War*, and with *Fade*, in 1988, moved into a new phase.

There was no question that Cormier had become the leading young adult author—and some critics felt that was too narrow a definition of his genius. Honors and awards were heaped on him repeatedly: New York Times Outstanding Book of the Year, American Library Association Young Adult Services Division Best Books, the ALAN Award from the Assembly of Literature for Adolescents of the National Council of Teachers of English, an honorary doctor of letters from Fitchburg State College. But best of all, from Cormier's point of view, were the many letters from young readers letting him know how important his books were to their lives.

When Fitchburg College established a Cormier archives on 3 May 1981 he was pleased but a little puzzled that anybody would want all his old papers. "It's nice, though, to have all those boxes out of the house," he said. "The closets were getting pretty full, and Connie was starting to complain."

3. At the Typewriter

"I love staying up during the night," Cormier wrote in a 1970 newspaper column. "This is when knowledge seems to arrive, when thoughts are lucid and clear, when the lyrics of the Stones . . . resound with additional meaning or when the poetry of Edwin Arlington Robinson sings with new music. . . . The small hours are the hours when the telephone doesn't ring, when the doorbell is mute, when traffic whispers along the street outside and nobody blows a horn. Nighttime doesn't really begin until 11 o'clock or so when I always make sure that I miss the nightly newscasts. I am not the least interested in news at that hour or even weather forecasts—let tomorrow and the world take care of itself. But I often indulge in the talk shows. . . . Television is only part of the magic of the night, halting for me at one o'clock when the deep night arrives, the hours of hush, a time to ponder imponderables, to entertain thoughts that the dazzle of daylight prevents. . . . Those are sweet moments, sitting quietly in the night, reading or listening to music or simply thinking—such a pleasure to let thoughts soar, limitlessly, it seems—and all the time the ones you love are asleep and safe under your roof."[1]

These "hours of hush" are Cormier's best working time. While the rest of Leominster sleeps, his characters come out and dance, and his plots move relentlessly toward their grim conclusions.

"Thank God for insomnia," wrote one reviewer. "I hope no one ever says to Robert Cormier: 'Sleep well.' "[2]

In the morning he is back at the typewriter for four or five more productive hours. His years of newspaper work taught him the discipline: "At seven o'clock in the morning you go to work, you're half asleep, and the deadline might be mid-morning, and there's the blank page, and you can't fake it. After years and years of this, now I have the ability to go from the easy chair to the typewriter when everything in the world cries out to me, 'Today I don't feel like writing; today I've got a good book; it's a lousy day—' And yet something brings me to that chair."[3]

Once the inertia has been conquered and he is immersed in an ongoing piece he works happily for four or five hours in his study without a door. The newsroom not only gave him discipline but also the ability to concentrate in the midst of ringing phone and doorbell, buzzing vacuum, and the comings and goings of his family. In the afternoon he goes for a walk or a drive, drops in to the *Sentinel* to visit old buddies, or roams around in the old neighborhood on French Hill. "I write until I lose perspective," he explains. "I come back and the problem is solved; the perspective is restored. You get so close to a thing, and then you have to draw away from it."[4]

Cormier is good friends with his subconscious, and its workings are a source of wonder and delight to him. "One of the joys of sitting down at a typewriter is finding out what's going to happen," he has said.[5] His characters have independent existences of their own. "When I'm at the typewriter (or driving the car or waiting in a supermarket line) and all the time thinking of characters, I am conscious of letting them come and go, allowing them to do all sorts of things. Some have staying power, others drift off. Some are not anticipated but arrive and hang around (like Amy Hertz or Emil Janza). I don't think of them as characters in a structured novel I am writing but simply as people that I'm watching grow and change. I don't sit down at the typewriter at nine o'clock in the morning and tell myself that I must write five or ten pages by noontime. I go to the typewriter to find out, say, what is going to happen today when young Adam Farmer goes into that lunchroom in Carver, New Hampshire, and confronts those three bullies. It may take five pages or ten pages or fifteen to find out. But finding out is the peculiar joy I encounter when I'm writing, although that same finding out sometimes leads me astray and cost me countless pages that are eventually discarded."[6]

The trigger that sets those characters in motion, that starts them moving purposefully into a story, is always an emotion. Sometimes a seemingly trivial incident, like Peter's return of the chocolates, can bring up strong feelings that resonate in Cormier's subconscious and initiate his need to try to find just the right words to create that same state in his readers. "The emotion sparks my impulse to write and I find myself at the typewriter trying to get the emotion and its impact down on paper," he has said. "The thing I'm trying to do is communicate with the reader—communicate the emotion I want him to feel. I sacrifice everything to that. I want to hit the reader with whatever emotion I want to portray, or whatever action will make it vivid."[7] Writers who cold-bloodedly survey the market, outline a plot and sell a book idea, and then sit down to flesh out a novel to meet a deadline may find Cormier's working methods naive. Yet it is his willingness to trust in his own deep, hidden knowing, to fling himself out into space at the typewriter, that is the source of much of the power of his work. (Of course, sometimes an emotion or a character beckons him down into a dead end. "That's when you have novels that fail within fifty or sixty pages," he observes without regret.)[8]

After the subconscious has had its playtime, he goes back and brings his fine craftsmanship to bear. "I write, then I cut and shift and change. It's like being a sculptor always chiseling away. You know the figure is there, the form and shape. You want to get it as close as you can to the figure in your mind."[9] This is nuts-and-bolts time. "At first when I sit down at the typewriter, I don't worry about syntax or fine writing. I try to capture a mood, an atmosphere, a scene or a character. And then I go back to find the exact phrase or word that arrests the action in the reader's mind." He looks for "words such as those good, galloping, active verbs which dance and jump from the page. I watch my adverbs. If I use too many I know my verbs are weak."[10]

"I love to rewrite. I love to tinker with the words. I hate to let novels go when they are done. One of my novels, *Take Me Where the Good Times Are*, I actually wrote over completely after it was all done and ready to go to the publisher. . . . I get pretty involved with the characters."[11] But new characters, new emotions boil up to take the place of those that are leaving, and "when I get to the end of a novel I'm already into another one."

"I like to be taken seriously and to have people discuss characters in my books as if they really exist, because they do exist for me."[12] But when critics and reviewers shift their focus from his actors to sweep aside the curtain and reveal the puppeteer at work, he grows self-conscious and uneasy. His modesty has something to do with this, but also there is an almost superstitious feeling that looking too closely at the magic gift of inspiration might make it disappear. "For a long time, I was reluctant to analyze my writing and grew uncomfortable when I encountered articles arguing certain aspects of it, the quality of realism, say, in *The Chocolate War*. I felt like one of those characters in a television cartoon who flies through the air until he becomes conscious of what he's doing and looks down in horror, loses the ability to fly, and plummets to the earth. Too much theorizing worries me. . . . It makes me feel as though I am looking into a mirror as I write."[13]

"I have to trick myself into writing a novel—and the trick is to convince myself that I'm not actually writing one . . . something between covers, frozen in print, a piece of merchandise, the subject of a contract, a package to be stamped and weighed and distributed, a book on a shelf in a store or a library. The idea of setting out to produce such a thing scares the daylights out of me."[14] "I don't sign contracts with publishing houses. I don't tell them when a novel will be done. I don't know myself."[15] Every book for Cormier is an unfolding adventure, not a marketable product. The pleasure for him is in the process, and the fact of publication later is secondary.

Interviewers often ask Cormier whether being published as a young adult author imposes limitations on his work. The only negative effects he will acknowledge are that labels cut him off from potential readers—adults and also young adults who resent having their reading categorized—and that "children's writers" are seen as second-class citizens by the literary establishment. At the typewriter he does not aim at an audience of any particular age. "I do not regard myself as a 'young adult' author. . . . I think any story or novel, if written honestly and without regard for a specific audience, will set off shocks of recognition across a broad range of readers."[16] "I always had in my mind an intelligent reader who likes me and will forgive me my trespasses and errors and go along with me. And thank goodness, that intelligent reader often turns out to be fourteen years old." He never lets himself be troubled about whether a particular passage is too difficult, too daring, too grim for young readers. "When a writer has to worry that way about his audience, that's death to all creative impulses."[17]

On the other hand, he is very aware of the teenager inside himself when he writes. "I've never been able to trace my own border crossings. I am eighteen forever and also 32 and 53 and 14 and 21—and I would not want it to be any other way."[18] His total recall of emotions from his past gives him sound rapport with teens. "It's not as if I sit at the typewriter and say, 'How does a kid feel?' I know how a kid feels."[19] "And I don't worry too much about trends or styles. I figure that if the emotions are right, the response will be there."[20] The response *is* there, judging from the myriad letters and phone calls he gets. The love affair is mutual; he is lavish in his praise: "There is no audience so responsive, so caring, so quick to be passionate about a book, so innocently critical and so marvelously appreciative."[21]

Cormier is a voracious reader and is quick to credit literary influences on his work. For a time, after his electrifying first encounter with Thomas Wolfe, he tried without success to imitate those torrents of words. Then he found the "lean clean prose of Ernest Hemingway"[22] and learned from him "what the simple word can do—the right word."[23] It was simplicity, too, that attracted him to William Saroyan. From mysteries, which he admits to reading "like popcorn," he absorbed a feeling for the structures of suspense.[24] John Le Carré and Graham Greene are also favorites.[25] But it was the newsroom where Cormier served his apprenticeship, and where he learned to write tight and true with accuracy and economy.

During his years as an editor at the *Sentinel* he indulged himself in a "human-interest column" that appeared regularly under the byline "John Fitch IV" from 1968 to 1978.[26] Occasionally he would review books or films that had taken his fancy, but mostly he jotted down passing observations on his thoughts about daily life in Leominster as he stood in the big bay window of his office and looked down at the passing bustle or strolled up Main Street with his eyes and ears open. He tried for small shocks of recognition, little connections among people and events and feelings. At first, under the heading "Man Having Fun at a Typewriter," the columns were often random collections of one-liners. Later columns more frequently were examinations of one theme, like the invocation to the night that opens this chapter, or a wistful piece about his sympathy for movie monsters. The tone is gentle humor, a bit ironic, a bit melancholy. (A collection of these columns, edited by Connie Cormier, is soon to be published by Delacorte under the title *And So On—*.)

The short stories are similar in flavor. Most of the seventy-five stories he produced during the years before his success as a young adult novelist are pleasant but misty. One looks in vain for the hard fist to the gut of the dark novels. A young soldier is gently rejected by a girl he has just met; a newsman's marriage falls apart on the same day that Kennedy's death comes over the teletype; a French-Canadian family delude themselves about a windfall of cash.

Although these were a steady market, Cormier in retrospect never found the form completely congenial. "I never liked writing short stories that much. They're very demanding and very difficult. A short story can't change your life, but a novel can. In a novel you can move around and create people and have a good time. You can't do that in a short story. Every word counts. You have to keep the forward thrust. You can't play with it. I haven't written a short story since *The Chocolate War*."

Critics have been puzzled by the apparent contrast between the

Cormier of the columns and short stories and the Cormier of the novels. Some have observed that there seems to be almost a schizophrenic split in his vision of the world.[27] He himself has acknowledged this duality: stung by criticism about the "depressing" quality of his later novels, he defended himself by pointing out that *Eight Plus One* shows readers "another Cormier."[28]

Actually, taken as a whole the short stories and the novels are not that dissimilar. It is an oversimplification to classify the first as warm and compassionate and the second as cold and grim. In both forms he writes in a minor key; in both he explores the inherent ironies of life with pity for his protagonists. True, some of the short stories have a humorous twist (as does *Take Me Where the Good Times Are*), but the laughter is always rueful.

The differences are primarily a matter of scale. The stories are ordinary, daily, and the pain is mixed with sweetness. But when the camera moves back in the novels to show the larger picture, the strangeness of dark, controlling forces appears on the horizon in a way that is explanatory rather than contradictory to the smaller events of the short stories. The characters in the novels are more tragic simply because we see the whole pattern, rather than a fragment, of their lives. The smaller vision is contained within the larger. Indeed, Cormier has recycled some of the incidents from the short stories into his novels: the arrogant girl at the bus stop, for instance.

It is also probably true that the demands of the smaller form for tighter control on the part of the author does not allow Cormier to draw on the depths of his subconscious. He cannot let go and allow the characters to go where they will, as he so loves to do in his novels. They must walk soberly on the ground the short path from here to there. The creative process cannot reach down deep enough to be in touch with the dark energy of Cormier's central vision.

What is this vision that has so fascinated and enraged critics? What exactly is it that Robert Cormier is trying to say? Many reviewers, speakers, and essayists have had a try at analyzing it. Some have settled for easy generalities. His themes, they say, are betrayal, vulnerability, guilt, paranoia, fear, and psychosis.

Others have groped for a nucleus in those ideas: "His novels deal with the struggle of the individual against often malicious, sometimes unidentified, external forces and stress the importance of self-reliance."[29] He is "particularly hard on authority," observed the *Boston Globe*.[30] The most common description of his worldview, and one that Cormier himself has used, is "the plight of the individual versus the system."

Millicent Lenz has made an elaborate argument for the theory that Cormier is depicting a dark, tragic world in order to imply the opposite—a bright, happy world. His books, she maintains, are "ironic" in that they are meant to instruct readers how *not* to act, so that their world will be the opposite of the world his characters have brought on themselves. She says: "so desolate a vision calls up a counter-vision of a possible better world—the world that lies within human will and choice to realize."[31]

Anne MacLeod, in an analysis that is even more perceptive, thinks that Cormier's central focus is political, in the broad sense of that word. "The typical adolescent novel is wrapped tightly around the individual and the personal; questions of psychological development and personal morality dominate the genre," she writes. "Cormier, on the other hand, is far more interested in the systems by which a society operates than he is in individuals. His novels center on . . . the political context in which his characters, like all of us, must live. . . . He has evoked a political world in which evil is neither an individual phenomenon nor a personality fault explainable by individual psychology, but a collaborative act between individuals and political systems which begins when the individual gives over to the system the moral responsibility that is part of being human. . . . I cannot discover that he wants to tell his readers that by recognizing their dangers they can escape them, and I do not think his books can be reduced to a positive statement about the protective virtue of political understanding." Perhaps the message can be summed up as "what you fail to understand about your world can destroy you, either literally or as a human being."[32]

MacLeod's reasoning is ingenious, and accurate as far as it goes. The problem is that she, like other critics, bases her conclusions on only three of Cormier's eight published novels. It is true that the system is the enemy in *The Chocolate War, I Am the Cheese*, and *After the First Death*. The political evil increases in power and scope with each book, from the authoritarian excesses of a parochial school to the authoritarian excesses of the world military conspiracy. But when we include Cormier's other novels in the question "Who is the enemy?" a different pattern emerges from the answers.

Isolating the central fixed point, the immovable factor, the solid wall against which the action crashes, is the key to understanding the fiction of Robert Cormier. It is tempting but not quite accurate to think of this force as "the enemy." In *A Little Raw on Monday Mornings* it is pregnancy against which good Catholic Gracie struggles. In *Take Me Where the Good Times Are* it is old age, and in both *Now and at the Hour* and *The Bumblebee Flies Anyway* it is death. But most revealingly, in the unpublished novel "In the Midst of Winter," the force is God Himself, the Holy Spirit that pursues the agnostic with implacable love until he finally surrenders.

The "enemy," then, is not necessarily evil. The unifying characteristic in all these manifestations of the concept can be neatly pinned down with the word "implacable." Unalterable, inflexible, inexorable—that which cannot be appealed to. What fascinates Cormier, the eternal question that draws him back again and again, is "How can we confront the utterly Implacable and still remain human?" His emotion centers on the individual made powerless, cut off from all recourse. Thus Cormier's plots often turn on the symbolic regaining of power through one supremely irrational but self-determined gesture.

Cormier recalls an incident from his childhood that is a metaphor, or perhaps one of the sources, for the rage he feels about helplessness at the hands of the Implacable. "They" had decided that he was to have his tonsils out, in spite of all his pleading and protests. So when the day came, off he was taken to the hospital. He was wheeled into the operating room, trying to make the best of the situation. A nurse, evidently having heard that he was in the church choir, said to him, "I understand that you sing—would you do us a song?" Pleased and flattered, he opened his mouth to let out the first notes, and instantly the anesthetic mask was clamped down over his face. Betrayal! He still feels angry when he remembers the moment. "They tricked me! I thought they loved me because I sang, and they tricked me. I'll never forget it. Authority sucks you in, and then—!" No matter how lovable or deserving or pitiful you are, there is no appeal. The Implacable has its own purposes.

In the light of Cormier's feelings about ultimate power, it is understandable that his attitude toward his own Catholicism is ambivalent. "My religion has been both a burden and a blessing," he admits. Few manifestations of earthly power are so absolute as that of the pope over devout Catholics. The authoritarianism of the nuns, as we have seen, was a misery to his childhood. But the Church has also been a comfort and a bulwark to him.

Cormier is a deeply moral man, in the finest sense. He cares profoundly about the world's pain and is scrupulous that his own daily actions help to erase rather than increase that suffering. This beauty of character probably comes naturally from the loving integrity of his personality, but he also is very much in touch with his Catholic conscience. "I was made aware of evil," he admits, "and I'm aware of it now. I mean, we constantly try to be good, and most of us are because of the lack of the opportunity to be evil. . . . But I'm aware all the time of trying to do the right thing, the good thing, and of often not doing it. As I've said, it's the sins of omission that hound me."[33]

He has come to terms with his religion since the era of Pope John XXIII opened the windows, and he now feels much more relaxed with his faith. "A theology of love," he calls it, contrasted with the "theology of fear" of his childhood.[34] It is this more mature understanding that soars over his writing as the spire of St. Cecelia's soars over French Hill. But his honesty will not allow easy comfort from theological slogans, as his plots will not allow contrived happy endings. There is no traditional "God talk" in his published novels, nor is there any specific religiosity.

The dedication page in *Bumblebee* reads: "To old pals Jude Thaddeus, Martin and Anthony and a new one, Max, with thanks." These are the saints to whom Cormier goes in his prayers. Jude Thaddeus, the saint of impossible cases. Martin, a black priest in South America. Anthony, who finds lost things. And Maximillian Kolbe, who gave up his life so a family could live, in a concentration camp in World War II. When a friend is in trouble or pain, Cormier will often promise, "I'll get my buddies on the job."

Power need not be implacable.

4. *The Chocolate War*

"They murdered him." The opening line of *The Chocolate War*. Three words that describe the whole movement of the plot. The process of "murdering" Jerry Renault is the subject; it remains only to tell who and why and how they felt about it. And what it meant.

On the surface the story is straightforward enough, moving along quickly in brief, intense scenes. We first see Jerry slamming through a football practice. He is a freshman at Trinity High School in Monument, and making the team is important to him, a small compensation for the recent death of his mother and the gray drabness of his life with his defeated father. The camera shifts to the stands; there we meet Archie, the villainous brains of the secret society called the Vigils. He is plotting "assignments" with his henchman Obie, cruel practical jokes to be carried out by selected victims. On the way home, Jerry is confronted at the bus stop by a hippie vagrant who challenges his passive conformity. Meanwhile, the malevolent Brother Leon, acting headmaster of Trinity, has called Archie into his office to break the traditional conspiracy of silence about the Vigils by asking for their help in the school chocolate sale. As Archie later discovers, Leon, in a bid for power while the headmaster is in the hospital, has overextended the school's funds to take advantage of a bargain in twenty thousand boxes of chocolates. Archie is delighted to have the vicious brother capitulate to him. Now we see Archie in action, as an inoffensive kid called The Goober is assigned to loosen every screw in a classroom so that it falls into debris the next morning at the first touch. But no assignment is complete until Archie has drawn from a box containing six marbles—five white and one black. If the black turns up—as it never has yet—Archie himself must carry out the assignment. But again the marble is white. Next we see Leon in action, tormenting a shy student with false accusations of cheating while the class watches tensely, then turning on the group to accuse them of condoning the cruelty by their silence. An even more vicious character is the bestial Emile Janza, who is in bondage to Archie over an obscene snapshot. Now the cast is complete and the action begins.

To show Leon where the power lies, Archie secretly assigns Jerry to refuse to sell the chocolates for ten days. Brother Leon is enraged but impotent as every day at roll call Jerry continues to answer "No." Suspecting a plot, Leon calls honor student David Caroni into his office and threatens to spoil the boy's perfect academic record with an undeserved F unless he reveals the secret. Terrified, Caroni tells him about the assignment. Finally the ten days are up, but Jerry, for reasons he only dimly understands, still continues stubbornly to refuse to sell the chocolates. Surreptitious approval for Jerry's stand begins among the other students, and for the first time he begins to understand the words on a poster he has taped in his locker: "Do I dare disturb the universe?" The sales begin to drop off. Leon, panicked, pressures Archie; Archie pressures Jerry before the Vigils, but Jerry clings to his resolve. Soon it becomes apparent that the power of both Leon and the Vigils will be destroyed by the failure of the chocolate sale. When Carter, the jock president of the Vigils, in frustration resorts to his fists to subdue a contemptuous assignee at a Vigils' meeting, Archie realizes Jerry's resistance must be destroyed utterly. The Vigils take charge of the chocolates, and under their secret management sales mount dramatically. With this turn of the tide, the school is caught up in the enthusiasm. Jerry is ostracized and tormented, first secretly by the Vigils and then openly by the whole student body. Finally Archie prods Emile

Janza to taunt Jerry into a fistfight, but characteristically Emile hires some children to do the actual beating. The Goober, in a belated show of support, decides to stop selling, but his gesture is futile. Soon the sale is over, and only Jerry's fifty boxes of chocolates remain. Archie conceives a diabolical scheme for final vengeance. Under cover of a supposed night football rally, he stages a "raffle" for the last boxes of chocolates. He offers Jerry "a clean fight" with Emile Janza, and Jerry, wanting desperately to hit back at everything, accepts. Only when he and Emile are already in the boxing ring are the rules explained. The raffle tickets are instructions for blows and the recipient is forbidden to defend himself. But now Carter and Obie come forward with the black box. Archie's luck holds; the marble is white. The fight begins as planned, but Emile's animal rage is quickly out of control, and the mob goes wild as he beats Jerry savagely. The carnage is stopped when one of the brothers arrives and turns out the lights, but it is too late for Jerry. Terribly injured and lying in The Goober's arms, he begs him not to disturb the universe, but to conform, to give in. An ambulance takes him away, and Archie, who has seen Brother Leon watching with approval in the shadows, is left triumphant.

The novel works superbly as a tragic yarn, an exciting piece of storytelling. Many young adults, especially younger readers, will simply want to enjoy it at this level, and Cormier himself would be the first to say that there is nothing wrong with that. A work of literature should be first of all a good story. But a work of literature also has resonance, richness, a broader intent than just the fate of the characters. For the reader who wants to dig a bit beneath the surface, there is a wealth of hidden meaning and emotion in *The Chocolate War*. How does Cormier achieve this atmosphere of dark, brooding inevitability? What are the overarching themes from which the events of the plot are hung? And, most of all, just what is the crucial thing that he is trying to tell us?

A look at Cormier's style in this book will show first of all the driving, staccato rhythms. The sentences are short and punchy, and the chapters are often no more than two pages. He uses dialogue to move the action quickly forward and to establish character and situation in brief, broad strokes. His technique is essentially cinematic; if he wants to make a psychological or philosophical point he does so visually with a symbolic event or an interchange between characters, rather than reflecting in a verbal aside. Tension is built by an escalating chain of events, each a little drama of its own. "Rather than waiting for one big climax, I try to create a lot of little conflicts," he explains. "A series of explosions as I go along."[1]

The point of view snaps back and forth from boy to boy in succeeding chapters, a more focused use of the technique called "omniscient observer." First we see Archie through Obie's eyes, then we are inside Jerry's head, then we watch Leon and The Goober squirm under Archie's gaze, then we are looking up at him from Emile's dwarfish mind, then we watch Brother Leon's classroom performance through Jerry's quiet presence, and so on. The variety of perspectives develops our understanding of the characters and reveals the complex interweaving of motivations and dependencies. The shift is unobtrusive but can be easily detected by a close look at the text. Less subtly, there are occasional tags that clue the reader to a change in voice: Brian Cochran and Obie, for instance, are inclined to think, "For crying out loud!," while Archie, among others, is addicted to the ironic use of the word *beautiful*. Cormier is too fine a writer, of course, to descend to imitation slang in order to indicate that this is a teenager speaking. Nothing dates a book more quickly than trendiness, as he learned from "The Rumple Country," and his understanding of the quality of adolescence goes far deeper than picking up the latest expression.

Much has been made of Cormier's imagery, and many essays and articles have been written on his metaphors and similes, his allusions and personifications. Sometimes it seems that Cormier is merely exercising his virtuosity for the reader: "his voice curled into a question mark," or "he poured himself liquid through the sunrise streets." But most of the time his metaphors are precisely calculated to carry the weight of the emotion he is projecting. Carter, about to tackle Jerry, looks "like some monstrous reptile in his helmet." Leon, thwarted, has "a smile like the kind an undertaker fixes on the face of a corpse." Jerry, happy, scuffles through "crazy cornflake leaves" but, sad, sees autumn leaves flutter down "like doomed and crippled birds." Jerry's father, preparing their loveless dinner, slides a casserole "into the oven like a letter into a mailbox." Sometimes the imagery is vividly unpleasant, as some reviewers have complained, but it is always appropriate to the intensity of the thing that Cormier is trying to say. There is a whole bouquet of bad smells in *The Chocolate War*, starting with Brother Leon's rancid bacon breath. The evening comes on as "the sun bleeding low in the sky and spurting its veins." Sweat moves like small moist bugs on Jerry's forehead. The vanquished Rollo's vomiting sounds like a toilet flushing.

Literary and biblical allusions, too, enrich the alert reader's experience of the novel. Shakespeare, the Bible, and the poetry of T.S. Eliot are the most obvious sources. "Cut me, do I not bleed?" thinks Emile, like Shylock. For Jerry, like Saint Peter, a thousand cocks have crowed. The quotation on the poster in his locker is from Eliot's "The Love Song of J. Alfred Prufrock." One reviewer has gone so far as to write an essay drawing parallels between Jerry and Hamlet, Archie and Iago.[2] Cormier denies building in this particular analogy, but admits that such references may come from his subconscious. The sophisticated reader, too, can absorb them subliminally, without conscious analysis.

Many of these allusions are not isolated flourishes, but fit together into larger structures of meaning. As one example, the Christian symbolism in *The Chocolate War* is an indication of the importance of the book's theme to Cormier. Before tracing that imagery, however, it is essential to clarify that the school itself is not part of this symbolism. It is a gross misunderstanding of the theme of the book to interpret it as an attack on parochial schools or the Catholic Church. If that had been Cormier's intention, it should be quite clear from his biography that he would have drawn on his childhood memories to picture a school where nuns, not brothers, presided. No, the fact that Trinity is a Catholic school is as irrelevant to the meaning of the story as that fact is irrelevant to the characters. But Cormier does use Christian symbolism to show the cosmic implications of the events he is relating. When Jerry refuses to sell the chocolates, the language suggests the Book of Revelation: "Cities fell. Earth opened. Planets tilted. Stars plummeted."[3] In the first chapter, the goal posts remind Obie of empty crucifixes, and in the last chapter, after Jerry's martyrdom, they again remind him of—what? In his graceless state, he can't remember. When Jerry is challenged to action by the hippie, the man looks at him from across a Volkswagen so that Jerry sees only the disembodied head. The image is John the Baptist, he who was beheaded by Herod after he cried in the wilderness to announce the coming of Christ. Archie's name has myriad meanings from its root of "arch": "principal or chief," "cleverly sly and alert," "most fully embodying the qualities of its kind"; but most significantly, the reference is to the Archangel, he who fell from Heaven to be the Fallen Angel, or Lucifer himself. The Vigils, although Cormier admits only to a connotation of "vigilantes," resonate with religious meaning. The candles placed before the alter in supplication are vigil candles, and a vigil is a watch on the night preceding a religious holiday. The members of the gang stand before Archie, who basks in their admiration like a religious statue before a bank of candles.[4] But most important, the understanding of the ultimate opposing forces of good and evil in *The Chocolate War* is a deeply Christian, or perhaps even a deeply Catholic, vision.

How does the theme of this book fit into Cormier's fascination for the nature of human confrontation with the Implacable? All of the three villians are vulnerable, and if they cannot quite be placated, they can at least be manipulated. They are quick to see each other's weaknesses and quick to take advantage of them for more secure positions of power. Leon has put himself in a shaky place by his overreaching ambition, and Archie sees him "riddled with cracks and crevices—running scared—open to invasion." Archie fears Leon's power over him as his teacher, and his domination of the Vigils is dependent on thinking up ever more imaginative assignments. And then there is the black box—a nemesis over which he has no control. Emile's weakness is his stupidity;

he is easily conned by Archie into believing in the imaginary photograph. So none of the three is an implacable, unconquerable force; all are subject to fears and weaknesses.

Why then does Jerry's lone refusal seem so very doomed from the beginning? Why does the contest seem so unequal; why does the action move so inevitably toward tragedy? The answer lies in the nature of what it is he is saying "no" to. What he is opposing is not Brother Leon, not Archie, not Emile, but the monstrous force that moves them, of which they are but imperfect human agents. The Goober gives it a name: " 'There's something rotten in that school. More than rotten.' He groped for the word and found it but didn't want to use it. The word didn't fit the surroundings, the sun and the bright October afternoon. It was a midnight word, a howling wind word." The word is *evil*.

The unholy trinity of Trinity are studies in the human forms of evil. Brother Leon, who as a priest is supposedly an agent of the Divine, has sold his soul for power, even down to his exultation in the small nasty tyrannies of the classroom. Cormier has said that he chose the name Leon, a bland, soft name, to match the brother's superficial blandness. "And so is evil bland in its many disguises," he adds.[5] Leon's appearance is deceptive: "On the surface, he was one of those pale, ingratiating kind of men who tiptoed through life on small, quick feet." "In the classroom Leon was another person altogether. Smirking, sarcastic. His thin, high voice venomous. He could hold your attention like a cobra. Instead of fangs, he used his teacher's pointer, flicking out here, there, everywhere." Leon's skin is pale, damp, and his moist eyes are like boiled onions or specimens in laboratory test tubes. When he blackmails Caroni into revealing Jerry's motivation, his fingers holding the chalk are like "the legs of pale spiders with a victim in their clutch." After he has demolished the boy, the chalk lies broken, "abandoned on the desk, like white bones, dead men's bones." The image that gradually accumulates around Leon is that of a hideous, colorless insect, a poisonous insect, crawling damp from its hiding place under a rock. Or perhaps he has emerged from even deeper underground, as Jerry suspects when he sees "a glimpse into the hell that was burning inside the teacher."

Archie is far subtler and will utimately, when he is an adult, be more dangerous, because he is not in bondage to ambition. True, he revels in the captive audience of the Vigils, but he is not really part of that or any political structure. "I am Archie" he gloats, Archie alone. For him, the pleasure is in building intricate evil structures for their own sake. "Beautiful!" he cries as Brother Eugene falls apart like the furniture in his room, as Leon squirms under the pressure of Jerry's refusal, as Jerry struggles ever deeper into the exitless trap Archie has made for him. Yet, Archie, too, is in hell, the hell of understanding only the dark side of human nature. "People are two things," he tells Carter. "Greedy and cruel." From this knowledge comes his strength, his ability to make anybody do anything. But it is bottomless emptiness. "Life is shit," he says without emotion.

Emile is the purest embodiment of evil. In him we see the horror of evil's essential quality: silliness. Emile loves to "reach" people. He giggles when he leaves a mess in the public toilet, when he secretly gives an already-tackled football player an extra jab, when he loudly accuses a shy kid of farting on a crowded bus. Essentially evil is pointless. Purpose and structure belong to goodness; evil can only turn back on itself in chaos. Archie and Leon have clothed their evil with intelligence and worldly power, but Emile's surrender to darkness is revealed in all its terrible nakedness. The others recognize his nonhumanity quite clearly. "An animal," they call him.

Archie is amused by Emile's simplicity but also chilled by the recognition of a kinship he is not willing to acknowledge. Emile, however, in his perverse innocence, easily sees that he and Archie are "birds of a feather," and that their differences are only a matter of intelligence. An even more terrible innocence is that of the children whom Emile recruits to ambush Jerry. "Animals," he calls them in turn, and they emerge crouching from the bushes to do his bidding like the twittering hordes of little devils in a painting by Hieronymus Bosch.

Both Archie and Emile have cross-wired their sexual energies into sadism. Emile wishes he could tell Archie how he sometimes feels "horny" when he does a particularly vicious thing. The sources of Archie's most maliciously creative ideas are found in his sexual energy, as Cormier made clear in a chapter that was never printed. In these deleted pages Archie, backed into a corner by thinking of Jerry's recalcitrance, attempts to masturbate, but his powerlessness against the situation renders him impotent. Finally he gets the glimmering of an idea—and an erection—and conceives the scheme for the boxing match that will destroy Jerry at the same moment that he achieves his climax. The chapter is stunning in its sensuality, but Cormier, on the advice of his editor and because he found he was reluctant to allow his own daughter to read it, removed it from the final manuscript.[6]

All three villians are completely devoid of any sense of guilt. Indeed, Archie often congratulates himself on his compassion. Brother Leon is all surface; his soul is hollow, and he is the one character whose interior monologue we never hear. Repentance is totally foreign to him. Emile is even a bit defensive at being defined as a bad guy. "All right, so he liked to screw around a little, get under people's skin. That was human nature, wasn't it? A guy had to protect himself at all times. Get them before they get you. Keep people guessing—and afraid."

In chapter 4 Brother Leon mentions that Archie's father "operates an insurance business." This one shred of information is all we know about Archie's background. What could the home life of such a monster be? For that matter, what parent could live with Emile? Does Brother Leon have an aged mother somewhere? What were they all like as children? The questions are intriguing but pointless. Cormier deliberately gives us no hint of the origins of their devotion to darkness. "People can't say Archie did this because he was a deprived child or he was a victim of child abuse. I wanted him judged solely on his actions."[7] To understand is to forgive, and to forgive real evil is to make alliance with it. To render these characters psychologically understandable would be to humanize them, to undermine their stature as instruments of darkness, and therefore to erase the theme of opposition to the Implacable.

For those who would turn their eyes away from the ultimate and prefer a smaller and more comfortable theme, Cormier has thoughtfully provided an alternative. It is possible to view the book as an examination of tyranny. The pattern overlaps but is not identical. Seen this way, the trinity has a different cast. There are three structures of misused power: the school, as headed by Brother Leon; the athletic department, as headed by the coach; and the mob, as headed by Archie. Each has a passive assistant to tyranny, characters who have decent impulses but are ineffectual because they lack the courage to act. Obie is Archie's reluctant stooge; Carter agrees with the coach's approval of violence; and Brother Jacques despises Leon but condones his actions by not opposing. Shadowy outlines of the government, the military, and the Church might appear in this interpretation.

The question ultimately turns back, no matter whether tyranny or absolute evil is the enemy, to "How can we resist?" If evil had inherent power, there would be no answer. But Leon, Archie, and Emile all find their power source in their victim's own weaknesses. Leon even plays contemptuously with it in the classroom, when he tells the boys that they have become Nazi Germany by their fearful silence. Emile has very early discovered that most people want peace at any price and will accept almost any embarrassment or harassment rather than take a stand or make a fuss. "Nobody wanted trouble, nobody wanted to make trouble, nobody wanted a showdown." Archie, too, has realized that "the world was made up of two kinds of people—those who were victims and those who victimized." But the moment Jerry, of his own volition, refuses to sell the chocolates, he steps outside this cynical definition. In that is the source of hope.

Jerry at first has no idea why he has said no. "He'd wanted to end the ordeal—and then that terrible *No* had issued out of his mouth." But Jerry's life has been "like a yawning cavity in his chest" since his mother's death. His father is sleepwalking through his days, a man for whom everything and nothing is

"Fine!," a pharmacist who once wanted to be a doctor and now denies even that such an ambition ever existed. Like Prufrock, he is too numb to live and too afraid to act. When Jerry looks into the mirror he is appalled to see his father's face reflected in his own features. The hippie and the poster dare him to disturb the universe, and when he finally says no he is taking a stand against far more than a chocolate sale. And it is Brother Leon himself who has taught Jerry that not to resist is to assist.

Jerry is the *only one* who has learned that lesson, and this is what makes his destruction inevitable. Evil is implacable and merciless to a lone hero, in spite of the folk myth to the contrary. But could it have turned out differently? What if the marble had been black? Or Jerry's first blow had knocked Emile out? But these would have been arbitrary tamperings by the author. Ironically, the key to the real triumph of good comes again from Brother Leon. If others had joined Jerry. . . . There are a number of places in the story where this might have happened. The Goober, of course, is often on the verge of acting on his friendship for Jerry, but in the end, like Hamlet, he only thinks, and doesn't act until too late. For a moment he even hopes that it will all end in a stalemate. The Goober speaks for all the others in wanting to avoid confrontation at any cost. Obie might have acted on his disgust for Archie: "I owe you one for that!" he thinks when pushed too far. In the end he settles only for hoping that fate will punish Archie with a black marble. Carter, too, might have used his simple strength to end it.

Any of these isolated actions might have started the group movement that would have saved Jerry and defeated Leon and the Vigils. Even without such a spur the school comes close to following Jerry's example at the midpoint in the sale. But the motivation is negative—they are tired of selling and selfishly individual—"let each one do his own thing." Without a conscious joining together for the good of all, they can easily be maneuvered separately back into doing the Vigils' will.

So here at last is Cormier's meaning. As one critic has written, "Jerry's defeat is unimportant. What is important is that he made the choice and that he stood firm for his convictions."[8] Only by making that gesture can we hold on to our humanity, even when defeat is inevitable. But there is more—when the agents of evil are other human beings, perhaps good can win if enough people have the courage to take a stand together. Evil alliances are built with uneasy mutual distrust, but only goodness can join humans with the self-transcending strength of sympathy and love.

5. The Dark Chocolate Controversy

A border of funeral black enclosed the review of *The Chocolate War* that appeared in the American Library Association *Booklist* on 1 July 1974, a few months after the book's release in April. "Whammo, you lose," proclaimed the heading, and the author, Betsy Hearne, the magazine's children's book editor, wrung her hands over what she perceived as "the trend of didactic negativity" in books for young people. While acknowledging Cormier's power, she deplored the darkness of the vision he used that power to portray: "a book that looks with adult bitterness at the inherent evil of human nature and the way young people can be dehumanized into power-hungry and blood-thirsty adults. . . . Cormier is good at building and playing on dread. With a powerfully stacked plot and see-through characters he manipulates readers into believing how rotten things are by loading the dice while pretending to play fair. See these regular old dice? Whammo, you lose."[1]

She was not alone in her shock. Although most of the critics were enthusiastic about Cormier's skill, only some of them were brave enough to praise his honesty. Mary K. Chelton in *Library Journal* was one of these. She called the book "unique in its uncompromising portrait of human cruelty and conformity."[2] Richard Peck, himself a highly regarded young adult author, was equally impressed with the theme. Writing in *American Libraries*, he said: "Too many young adult novels only promise an outspoken revelation of the relevant. *The Chocolate War* delivers the goods. . . . Surely the most uncompromising novel ever directed to the '12 and up reader'—and very likely the most necessary. And anyone looking for a pat triumph of the individual had better avert his eyes. . . . The young will understand the outcome. They won't like it, but they'll understand."[3] Theodore Weesner of the *New York Times* was specific in his praise: "masterfully structured and rich in theme; the action is well crafted, well timed, suspenseful; complex ideas develop and unfold with clarity. . . . Written for teen-agers but a strong read for adults," he declared, and—prophetically—"an ideal study for the high school classroom."[4]

Some other critics completely missed the point. *Publishers Weekly*, the bible of the book industry, warned that the novel was "bound to cause controversy and no little resentment, especially among Catholics. . . . Its impact is weakened by the author's excess bitterness."[5] A few reviewers faulted Cormier for his lack of character development, not realizing that this was an integral part of his scheme. The English children's book review magazine, *Junior Bookshelf*, delivered the most vitriolic opinion: "This may be a brilliantly written tour de force but despite the publisher's claim it is no more a children's book than is *The Exorcist*. . . . *The Chocolate War* depicts a life without hope in which boys prey upon each other like prohibition gangsters, masturbate in the lavatory and drool over girlie magazines. It presents in one neat package all the most repellent aspects of the American way of life. Here in embryo are the forces of commercialism, of corruption, of sadism and the triumph of the beast. If you are an adult and an American it may shock you out of your complacency but English children will at the best be confused and at the worst enjoy it as a sadistic spectacle."[6] The *New Statesman* gave up entirely on a serious verdict and settled for translating the plot into current British slang: "Brother Leon, most greasy of eminences, in dead shtuck unless he off-loads his whole consignment of chockies . . ."[7]

But Peter Hunt of the *Times Literary Supplement*, the publication that is the pinnacle of world literary opinion, recognized the book's stature immediately. "A tour de force of realism. . . . If you must judge suitability, read the first two chapters; if you would judge a rather remarkable achievement . . . , read the whole."[8] After the dust had settled from the first impact, the literary establishment agreed. The *New York Times Book Review* awarded it a place on its annual list of Outstanding Books, and the Young Adult Services Division of the American Library Association chose it as one of their Best Books for Young Adults for 1974. Sales were impressive; in 1975, its first year in paperback, it went through three printings.[9] Young people devoured it, completely untroubled by the controversy.

But critics, teachers, and librarians continued to be uncomfortable with this lumpy package that Robert Cormier had handed them. Peter Hunt in the *Times Literary Supplement* had put his finger on the immediate cause when he said "Cormier's stock in trade is . . . to stand clichés (and our clichéd responses) on their heads and kick them, hard."[10] In a number of ways, *The Chocolate War* jarred expectations. Superficially, it looked to some older readers like a standard school story, the kind of tale about boyish pranks right under the headmaster's nose that had begun with *Tom Brown's Schooldays*. But with such an ending? To other more sophisticated readers it evoked the beloved American myth of the lone heroic refusal—*Billy Budd, From Here to Eternity*, the triumphant showdown at High Noon. Except that this showdown wasn't triumphant. And for those who were already familiar with patterns in young adult literature, Cormier's preoccupation with the universal rather than the personal was disorienting, and the lack of helpful adults and a happy ending violated a sacred tradition. As Donald Gallo said later, "somebody had challenged the status quo. Not just Jerry Renault, but Robert Cormier. *Robert Cormier had disturbed the universe of young adult books*!"[11]

It is important to remember that, as far as the critics were concerned, Cormier had come out of nowhere; he was a complete unknown to the world of juvenile fiction. It had been almost ten years since he had published a novel of any kind, and fifteen years since the flurry of critical excitement over *Now and at the Hour*. His three adult novels were out of print and virtually forgotten.

So it is no wonder that, when confronted by *The Chocolate War* with no other writings to put it in perspective, many critics overreacted and saw only bleak hopelessness where Cormier had intended an uncompromising but therapeutic honesty. And they worried about the effect on young people.

While the official opinion makers of the literary elite argued the book's meaning in polite essays, a few amateur critics waded in with unsophisticated zeal in other arenas. They knew *The Chocolate War* disturbed them, but they lacked the objectivity to analyze why, and so they, as would-be censors often do, justified their attack by flailing away with vague and unwarranted references to violence, sex, and "bad language." And even worse, they sometimes tried to prevent other people, particularly young people, from reading this book that they personally found objectionable.

In the summer of 1976 Connie Manter assigned *The Chocolate War* to the freshmen who would soon be entering her ninth-grade humanities and communication class in Groton, Massachusetts. "We hoped that it would be a springboard for discussion; since all the students were coming to the class from different backgrounds, the book would be the one thing the students would have in common," she later explained. "The book is structurally sound. It is a good example for plot sequence and it shows character development. And after we selected the book, we learned that the author lived nearby, and we thought that if he could address the class then it would be a human experience that we could not duplicate."

One or two mothers in the town disagreed. After glancing through the book their teenagers were reading for school, they went straight to the telephone and complained to school committeeman Andrew Zale. They had chosen their man well. By the time school opened in mid-September feelings had grown so intense that it was necessary to call a town meeting to air the matter. Nearly 150 people came to hear the fireworks. Zale presented his case. *The Chocolate War*, he argued, "is on the whole a depressing text which casts school authority in a completely adverse position to the students of the school and contains a wearisome abundance of violence and disruption coupled with veiled references to less than wholesome sexual activities. Also included is the figure of a member of a Christian denomination in a totally evil light." He proposed that the community establish a curriculum and textbook review committee to act as an authority in keeping such books out of the hands of students. Other members of the school committee rebuked Zale for his proposal. Connie Manter, the school librarian, and even some parents spoke out in favor of the book, but the most telling piece of testimony was a letter written by two students from Manter's class, Brett Rock and Mark Reeves, and signed by thirty-eight others. "A high school student does not have to open a book to read far worse things than *The Chocolate War*. Any trip to a public restroom will expose him to far more obscene written material. The book has a good story to tell. The supposed immoral statements are there to tell part of the story. You cannot protect us from hearing such things unless you lock us up. We do not think *The Chocolate War* could possibly make us challenge the authority of our parents and teachers. The students who are disrespectful toward their parents and teachers did not get that way by reading a book such as *The Chocolate War*."[12] The audience and the school board, except Zale, gave overwhelming support to keeping the book in the classroom.[13]

Later, when Cormier himself visited Manter's class he learned that there was a postscript to the incident. "The teacher said that when the students decided in the classroom to circulate a petition supporting the novel, one student stood up and said: 'Everyone in this class should sign the petition.' Another student stood up to say: 'Wait. If we insist that everybody signs this petition, then we'd be doing what happens in *The Chocolate War*. Let's not pressure anybody to sign.' The teacher said that this thrilled her. It made all the dispute and controversy worthwhile because the students had learned something from the novel and translated it into action."[14]

Other schools also had to fight to retain *The Chocolate War*, no matter how valuable they had found it. In Irmo, South Carolina, three teachers wrote a long letter to the principal carefully outlining the reasons he should not proceed with his decision to remove the book from the tenth-grade reading list. They praised it as a tool for teaching literary devices, but, more important, they praised its relevance to their students' lives. "Jerry, the main character, searches for an identity by deciding to resist peer pressure in his attempt to stand for *something*. Daily we observe our fifteen-year-old students following the same search and demonstrating the same behavior though not in such a dramatic way as Jerry chooses. . . . Some of the most interesting class discussions center around the way the students in the novel react to authority and the abuse of authority by adults. Our students almost overwhelmingly disapprove of the cruelty which is exhibited both by the teachers and the students in this novel."[15]

In Lapeer, Michigan, Nancy Devaney acted as spokesperson for Parents for Basic Education, a group that had organized during a controversy over a proposed sex education program. She and her followers, she testified before the Lapeer school board in December 1980, had been "working with" the school on textbook and supplementary reading material selection. The state board of the Moral Majority had offered to help with their project. "Our concern," she worried, "is that teachers have been making decisions on their own." The group's aim was the removal of books like *The Chocolate War*, which Devaney said contained "profanity for profanity's sake. I personally find it very offensive. There's a very explicit homosexual encounter." (Presumably she was referring to the scene in which Emile, coached by Archie, goads Jerry into a fight by accusing him of being "a fairy.") She went on: "We have a high moral standard for our family. Blasphemy offends my faith." The board asked for a review of the policy on book selection, and Devaney settled in to wait it out.[16] At about the same time an objection form had been filed at the public library by another citizen, describing the book as "totally immoral, lewd, and unacceptable for any intelligent person" and "suggestive, approving vandalism, homosexuality, immorality."[17]

Yet another controversy took place in Proctor, Vermont, in December 1981. There the Proctor School Board rejected, three to two, a request from several parents to remove the book from a ninth-grade English course. The parents considered it "too depressing and detrimental to attitudes and values of students." One of the three parents who filed the formal complaint said, "I thought it was hostile and totally disgusting. To show that evil triumphs is kind of sick to me." The board, however, decided: "The overall theme, philosophy and quality of writing makes it worthwhile reading," although they did remind the parents that they had the right to choose alternative classroom reading for their own children.[18]

It is important to stress that these were isolated incidents. The large majority of teachers who used the book in classes found that their students enjoyed it and found it deeply provocative, and parents and school authorities recognized the excellence of their choice. As Richard Peck had said in his review, "anyone banning this book for its locker-room-realistic language is committing a crime against the young."[19]

Meanwhile, the critics continued to discuss it in print in a more intellectual and less pragmatic fashion. Even after Cormier had published two more books, *I Am the Cheese* in 1977 and *After the First Death* in 1979, his opponents merely broadened their apprehensions about his darkness, although *The Chocolate War* remained the primary target. In July 1979 *Newsweek* printed an appreciative article by Tony Schwartz.[20] In the following weeks, letters from two readers took Cormier to task for his "unremitting pessimism." "Kids desperately need hope," wrote a reader from Oregon. "Despair is the most prevalent adolescent malady; suicide is the third highest cause of death for teenagers. I question promoting Cormier's messages that evil always triumphs and that the most heroic efforts will be crushed brutally; these may be dangerous for inexperienced people already in doubt about their chances of survival."[21] Another letter, from (significantly) Groton, Massachusetts, asked "why we have a generation of teenagers so accustomed to violence that they no longer squirm" at Cormier's novels.[22]

But Cormier had no lack of distinguished defenders. The English critic Pelorus, for instance, writing in *Signal*, called *The Chocolate War* a book that "every young person will have to read." He summed up the theme perceptively: "I would argue, and I fancy Cormier would too, that the real point of his book is to cause young readers to see the result of certain kinds of human behavior and to opt not for the hopeless end that the logically worked-out image presents, but for just the opposite."[23]

The two most lively sets of literary controversies were those generated by an article by Norma Bagnall in *Top of the News*, Winter 1980, and by an opinion column by Elizabeth G. Knudsen in *Wilson Library Bulletin*, September 1981. Bagnall, a teacher of English at Texas A & M University, titled her article "Realism: How Realistic Is It? A Look at *The Chocolate War*." "To portray things from the brutal or dark side only . . . is no more realistic than presenting only those sweet and idealistic stories of an earlier age," she began. Although she acknowledged that Cormier had probably written honestly from his own point of view, she argued that *The Chocolate War* presented a distorted picture of reality because there were no adults worth emulating in the story. "Jerry is the only decent kid, and he is victimized by his peers, with the cooperation of school officials. Only the ugly is presented through the novel's language, actions, and imagery; goodness and honor are never rewarded. Love and concern for other people is ignored, and hopelessness pervades the entire story." Bagnall was particularly offended by what she called the "ugly language" in the book. "I don't think it is necessary for a writer for young adults to feed back to them their own slang any more than it is necessary for a writer for five-year-olds to include the bathroom language he or she knows five-year-olds use and find titillating." The imagery, too, she termed "deliberately ugly" and she listed a number of examples. The suggested alternatives to Jerry's defeat that Cormier had embedded in the narrative, the turnings in the plot that might have led to a happier ending, Bagnall perceived as foreshadowing, and felt tricked that these hints had not led to a cheerful outcome. Although she granted that the novel was "brilliantly structured and skillfully written," she concluded that it was unsuitable for adolescent reading because "we can teach hopelessness to our young if they are taught that no matter how hard they struggle they cannot win. This story teaches that hopelessness."[24]

Top of the News (now *Journal of Youth Services in Libraries*), the magazine in which Bagnall's article was published, is the official periodical of the American Library Association for children's and young adult librarians. In the next issue, Betty Carter, a school librarian from Houston, and Karen Harris, an associate professor of library science at the University of New Orleans, answered Bagnall's attack. They pointed out that she had missed the metaphorical level of the story and gave a number of examples from Cormier's figurative language to prove that "its greater concerns are with the nature and functioning of tyranny. While it demonstrates the inability of a decent individual to survive unaided in a corrupt and oppressive society, it does not imply that such defeat is inevitable." Bagnall's assessment of the book as unrealistic because "only the ugly is presented" they felt had also missed the point. "Literary realism is not journalistic reporting," they wrote. "Novelists . . . choose particular elements of the world—distill, concentrate, and juxtapose them in such a manner as to illuminate a particular facet of the human condition. . . . If Cormier chooses to concentrate on the 'worse world,' he is exercising a literary privilege claimed by many major writers since Sophocles." Rather than feeling that *The Chocolate War* was unsuitable for teenagers, Carter and Harris felt that its message was valuable learning for the young: "The reason Jerry was not saved was because he stood alone. But he need not have been alone, as Cormier states clearly. . . . Robert Cormier does not leave his readers without hope, but he does deliver a warning: they may not plead innocence, ignorance, or prior commitments when the threat of tyranny confronts them. He does not imply that resistance is easy, but he insists it is mandatory."[25]

The following autumn, Jay Daly took exception to Bagnall's views in an article titled "The New Repression," also printed in *Top of the News*. Although Bagnall had not said so, Daly worried that her intent had been to endorse suppressing the book. He, too, felt that she had missed the point in her definition of realism, and had shown a lack of trust in the good sense of young people. Daly was not worried that young people would rush out and commit suicide because "they are taught that no matter how hard they struggle they cannot win," as Bagnall had said. Rather, he took comfort in observing that "they respond to the novel as humans, not English teachers, and apparently continue to believe that life is worth living."[26]

A similar heated exchange was touched off by an opinion column titled "Is There Hope for Young Adult Readers?" by freelance writer Elizabeth G. Knudsen. It was published in *Wilson Library Bulletin*, a magazine that has wide respect and readership from public librarians. Knudsen began with a quotation from *The Chocolate War* to the effect that "life was rotten, . . . there were no heroes, really, and . . . you couldn't trust anybody, not even yourself." In the first paragraph she adds two others: "People are two things: greedy and cruel" and "The world was made up of two kinds of people—those who were victims and those who were victimized." These statements she uses to show the "corruption and hopelessness" of the book, as if they were Cormier's own convictions. What Knudsen fails to indicate is that the three quotations are from the mouths of Archie and the disillusioned Caroni, and illustrate the state of the souls of those characters, not the state of Cormier's philosophy of life. Like Bagnall, Knudsen perceived the book's message as negative, although she recognized that "it is not possible—any more than it would be desirable—to hide evil from young adult readers. What is disturbing is not evil itself, but the fact that ugliness, frustration, and fear often end up sounding like the only reality." In this simplistic interpretation, Knudsen seemed to feel that *The Chocolate War* and other young adult novels say nothing about "courage, self-reliance, honesty, endurance, and faith," qualities that she stressed were needed by modern children, because "if their lives are miserable and frustrating, if the world around them is a shambles, the last thing young readers need to fill their imaginations is more of the same."[27]

Readers of *Wilson Library Bulletin* filled the letters page with responses for the next four months. Several overreacted by jumping to the conclusion that Knudsen was recommending that the books she had named be censored. A few letters supported Knudsen's plea for more "uplifting" subjects. But most respondents eloquently defended the ability of young people to understand and grow from the experience of reading *The Chocolate War*. Renee Hoxie wrote: "Let's not make futile attempts at conning young adults with a false sense of security in happy endings."[28] Jack Forman of San Diego State University Library felt that the novel was distinctly therapeutic in helping adolescents come to terms with the world.[29] And Mel Rosenberg, the Coordinator of Young Adult Services for Los Angeles Public Library, wrote a straight-talking letter, pointing out that "*The Chocolate War* is cautionary and compels the reader to ask the question: 'Do I have the stuff to be that kind of hero, to stand out against the crowd and take the consequences?' Few of us do, but many of us have to find out if we can—it's a tough part of growing up. What bothers me is that a first-rate piece of work keeps taking its lumps for its less-than-sunny view of the human soul. . . . *Moby Dick* has been around for quite a while now, and life on the Pequod makes Trinity High School look like Eden."[30]

The emotional and fairly unsophisticated nature of both controversies could be summed up by a sentence from the review written by the English critic Pelorus for *Signal* magazine: "It seems to me that too many children's book 'professionals' . . . still work on the assumption that literature makes people better only so long as the books themselves show a life, however unreal, which is the 'better' they want children and young people to be."[31] A great deal of fine talk was wasted on questions and issues that could have been simply solved by going directly to teenagers themselves, or by listening to what Cormier had said quite plainly in various interviews. Because high school kids, as *Boston* magazine observed, "do not flinch from the cold and terrible truths that Robert Cormier sticks in their faces like loaded guns."[32] In other interviews, Cormier said, "I still get letters from kids saying that what I wrote about in *The Chocolate War* is mild compared with what's going on in their schools."[33] "Kids take the terrible things that happen in my fiction easier than adults do. They ask me to explain something but they're never aghast."[34] "Kids today aren't cynical, but they can't stand phoniness. . . . All is not right with the world and the good guys don't always win; and they know it."[35] "Now, I've had letters from kids who are just heartsick over what happened to certain characters, but they don't oppose the endings on the grounds that they were unrealistic or that reading them was bad for them."[36]

Much of the adult reaction to *The Chocolate War* can, in the final analysis, be blamed on the ending. Not only does evil prevail, but—and here is the bit that sticks in the craw—the lone dissenter explicitly repudiates his whole struggle. Again Cormier's words illuminate a difficult point. Jerry, he has said, is "apparently" defeated.[37] A whole world of possibilities lies in that word. In a letter to the students of the Cohen Hillel Academy, he said it in another way: "To write a book in which the evil is victorious is not to condone it."[38]

Cormier has been bemused by the controversies. "You know, the funny thing about writing is that it is such a private act and it becomes such a public thing," he says.[39] To frequent questions about the ending of *The Chocolate War* he pleads inevitability. He often uses a compelling metaphor: once the iceberg has ripped the *Titanic*, the ship must sink. The rest of the story is just working out the details on the way to the end. He stood by the inevitability of Jerry's bleak defeat, even when three publishers rejected the book because of the ending. "I knew that in my mind the curve of the story was to build and then go down. And I had this crazy image in my mind of trying to fix up the ending to make it go up—'zip'—which seemed untrue, but it was tempting."[40] But when the chips were down, he stuck by his convictions. "A happy ending attached to a novel whose flow and tone and development is downbeat fatally flaws the work," he maintained.[41]

In the end, with Cormier it all comes down to a matter of integrity. "As long as what I write is true and believable, why should I have to create happy endings? My books are an antidote to the TV view of life, where even in a suspenseful show you know before the last commercial that Starsky and Hutch will get their man. That's phony realism. Life just isn't like that."[42] And to those who accuse him of celebrating hopelessness, he has a challenge, the plain message of *The Chocolate War*. "If you're going to fight this kind of thing, you've got to be collectively good," he says simply.[43] There *is* hope—but we must create it for ourselves.

6. *Beyond the Chocolate War*

"And then what happened?" The question that is put to rest at the end of a good story. But a question that, after a while, revives and tugs enticingly when an author has created characters that live their own lives beyond that particular set of events. "What happened to Jerry? And Archie?" young readers of *The Chocolate War* asked Cormier continuously. "And how about Tubs Caspar? Did he buy the bracelet for Rita?" Privately Cormier himself also wondered, especially about Obie. How had the dark days of the chocolate war changed him and the others at Trinity? And then what happened?

So, eleven years later, Cormier began to play around at the typewriter to find out. He conjured up the characters again and let them show themselves in new scenes. They had a lot to say, he found. "The book was much longer than I wanted it to be, simply because in the first version I wanted the people to go their way," he told editor Anita Silvey in an extraordinary two-part interview that appeared in the *Horn Book* magazine in March/April and May/June 1985.[1] "The hundreds of discarded pages for *Beyond the Chocolate War* fill a huge cardboard box."[2]

He pared and refined and distilled. The result is a work that in close analysis reveals itself as complex and dense, but on first reading has the spare and compelling clarity of great storytelling. The plot is an intricate delight of glittering illusions, magic tricks and surprises, yet paradoxically it moves with the utter simplicity and inevitability of absolute truth. The reader has no trouble at all keeping track of the more than a dozen major characters. The pacing is breathlessly irresistible. Unanswered questions and unresolved tensions layer from scene to scene as the characters collide in a rich choreography of shifting expectations, allegiances, and perceptions. Cormier revealed to *Horn Book* how he achieved this tension: "You have a rubber band that you keep pulling and pulling and pulling, and just at the moment of snapping you release it and start another chapter and start pulling again."[3]

It is the paradox of surprise and inevitability that is the chief pleasure of the book. In spite of all the unexpected jolts around each corner of the plot, the overwhelming experience for the reader is a sense of rightness. We know these characters, and this is just what they *would* do, just what *would* happen. We knew it all the time—except we didn't, until Cormier told us. As Tubs Caspar says to Obie, when he asks what happened when Rita didn't get her bracelet: "You know what happened." And when Tubs, as we were always sure he would, comes to Archie's attention as a natural victim, the assignment—to gain twenty pounds—is a perfect fit. The surprise is our sudden recognition of the inevitability of that fit.

The question that immediately comes to mind about any sequel is whether it can stand alone. Must the reader have experienced the chocolate war to be able to follow the action of *Beyond the Chocolate War*? In a limited sense, no. Cormier has dutifully written in all the events that went before, so that a newcomer can pick up the thread of the narrative. But the real heart of the story lies in the emotions and the characters, and these it is hard to grasp fully from a synopsis. The deeply satisfying inevitability of the action is rooted in our prior understanding of the actors. Indeed, so closely are the books linked as cause and result that perhaps the real question is whether they are two halves that should be published between the same covers.

Still, for the new reader Cormier needed a new character, someone who also needed to be told what went on last term. His name begins the first sentence of the book: "Ray Bannister started to build the guillotine the day Jerry Renault returned to Monument." A lapel-grabber of an opening, and one that sets up appropriately sinister expectations. A guillotine means an execution. Whose? Having gotten our attention, Cormier immediately denies everything with the second sentence: "There was no connection between the two events." But we know there's going to be. Especially when, in the last sentence of the chapter, Ray protests too much: "And as he told Obie later: Honest, he'd never heard of Jerry Renault or Archie Costello or any of the others." Cormier had explained in another context, "I think Chekhov said it—if you have a rifle on the mantel in the first act, it must be fired by the last act."

The important thing to remember about *this* guillotine is that it is an illusion. It cuts, and it doesn't cut. Cormier plays with our uncertainty about its nature and thus sets us up for the whole bag of magic tricks that he will perform in *Beyond the Chocolate War*. "Are you sure it's fool-proof?" asks Obie.

"Is anything really sure in this world?" Ray counters. The guillotine casts a tall dark shadow. All the while the story is unfolding in the halls of Trinity we are aware of Ray at home building the instrument of execution. Cormier has even given us in this first chapter a capsule preview of what the guillotine's final role will be, as Ray imagines himself performing for the student body: " 'May I have a volunteer from the audience?'—and hearing the guys gasp with astonishment as the blade fell, seeming to penetrate the volunteer's neck."

Ray is basically a simple soul, a carpenter. He likes to work with his hands, to sail his skiff. Although the deviousness of the magician would seem to be a foreign role to someone so straightforward, he finds its secrecy congenial because he is a private person, a natural loner. In the first chapter we see Monument through Ray's eyes, and the simile is drawn from his loneliness and boredom: "like a movie set from one of those old late-night films about the Depression." Trinity seems to him in his innocence to be "not wicked but only unfriendly and suffocatingly small." For us, who have come to know it as a whole dark world, his perception is ironic, as is his description of the brothers as "those strange people who wore stiff white collars but weren't quite priests yet weren't quite like ordinary men." His simplicity makes him immune to the evil at Trinity—"that Vigils stuff" only puzzles him. His name—meaning "a limited beam of light"—is a significant symbol. Cormier's first title for the book was "In the Darkness," a phrase that ends *The Chocolate War* and describes the condition of the world afterward. Ray's sunny wholesomeness is a bit of light in that darkness, and even when he is maneuvered into becoming the executioner, his simple good sense, in the form of the safety catch, deflects the ultimate moment of evil.

This first chapter is written in a rather flat narrative (as contrasted with the vivid scene on the football field that opens *The Chocolate War*). The effect is like a prologue, a statement before the real action begins that establishes the unanswered question of the guillotine. That done, Cormier the conjurer sweeps aside the curtain, and here we are back at Trinity, plunged with a shock of glad recognition into the familiar scene of a Vigils meeting. It is fall term, and at first glance everything looks the same—Carter with his gavel, Archie plotting an Assignment. But things have begun to change. Obie and Carter are restless and distracted. There are some new people in the darkened room—the sophomore Bunting and his henchmen Cornacchio and Harley.

The memory of the chocolate war hangs over the whole student body like a bad dream. It has made differences in the lives of the people we know from last term. Not surprisingly, Brother Leon has been appointed headmaster after the retirement of the former head. After all, this is what the chocolate sale was all about. Not a surprise either is the fact that Leon has had the decent Brother Jacques transferred. Brother Eugene, we learn later, has died from the mental and physical disruption that began with the collapse of his beloved Room Nineteen. Jerry Renault has been in Canada recovering, but is now back home, although not at school. Emile Janza is the same, or maybe even worse—a little heavier, a little more menacing, a little more of a brute. He and Archie seem untouched by the grim holocaust of last term. But Obie and Carter, Jerry and his friend The Goober, David Caroni—the passage of evil has left them struggling in its wake.

It is Obie whom Cormier sees as the protagonist of *Beyond the*

Chocolate War. "A tragic figure" he has called him, and the instrument of revenge.[4] Obie has lost everything by his devotion to Archie: his high school years, his own potential, his self-respect. Before the story is over, he has even lost the salvation of his love for Laurie Gundarson, because she is repelled by his connection with the Vigils. Pathetically, he tries to define himself to her, when she asks about the secret society, as "one of the good guys," but the name he gives himself as Ray's partner in the magic act is closer to the truth: "Obie the Obedient." When Archie forces him to face his identity as "a selector of victims" and perhaps even a murderer, he sees with horror that he has misplaced the blame all along. The face of evil is not Archie's but his own. "You could have said *no* anytime, anytime at all. But you didn't. . . ."

Here again is the theme of *The Chocolate War*, made even more explicit. Evil must be resisted collectively, but collective resistance begins with one *no*. Cormier spelled it out for the *Horn Book*: "The power of the leader comes from those who allow themselves to be led."[5] Each of the other characters provides variations on this theme.

Carter makes a gesture of resistance but it is misdirected, too late and too weak; he ends up being destroyed by it. The aftermath of the chocolates has left him unmoored, unanchored, and he blames Archie. "The tragedy of Carter's senior year was the ban on boxing imposed by Brother Leon. Carter had been captain of both the boxing team and the football squad. With the boxing team disbanded and the football season a distant memory, he was now captain of exactly nothing. His simple claim to distinction these days was his presidency of the Vigils. And as president he had to respond to Archie, play his games, shadowbox with words." He has to do something to reestablish his manhood. The big, beefy varsity guard is more decent and sensitive than anyone had suspected. When Archie plans a caper that will humiliate the bishop, Carter is appalled at the attack on the representative of goodness. He turns his outrage into action—but the wrong action. Instead of confronting Archie he writes an anonymous letter to Brother Leon, thus becoming a traitor. Archie makes him pay dearly by demolishing the two pillars of his self-respect: honor and pride.

The trophies Carter is so proud of winning for Trinity are stolen from the hall case and replaced with a little ceramic toilet. His pride is further ravaged when he must make a groveling confession to Archie, and when he almost betrays Obie's guillotine scheme to him as a bargaining point, he realizes that he has lost his honor in becoming a traitor a second time. A half-hearted gesture of resistance that does not directly confront the source of evil can backfire.

David Caroni, too, has misdirected his resistance. "Kill yourself and you also kill the world," he thinks as he pours the hot bath and lays out the razor blade. Ben (in *After the First Death*) and Barney (in *The Bumblebee Flies Anyway*) would have agreed. But at the last minute Caroni finds it is not enough; he must take Brother Leon with him into death more directly. David's opposition to evil becomes obsession and madness, out of proportion to the offense. Because Brother Leon has given him an F, he puts a knife to his throat. Even we, who know the extent of all Leon's evil doings, don't want a revenge like this. There is no justice in it; it is too much. As Brian Cochran thinks, "He wouldn't wish for Leon to be killed or wounded, but a good scare would be terrific." Caroni fails, and says *no* by ending his own life.

Leon does eventually get his just deserts, in a way that is completely appropriate. In this book he appears primarily as an antagonist for Archie, rather than as an agent of his own evil doings. But Leon of the moist milky eyes is still loathsome enough. In his new role as headmaster he has affected a repulsively mod style, with sideburns down to his earlobes. "He wore a silver chain, from which dangled a cross so fancy that you had to squint to make certain it was a cross." A diabolical symbol: the man of God who is not a man of God wears a cross that is not a cross. Again, as in *The Chocolate War*, he is the one character whose interior monologue we never hear—pure unexplained evil. It would have been pleasant if he had not been quite so brave under Caroni's knife, if he had blubbered a bit more. But when he stands pompously before the students of Trinity and tries to transfer the guilt for Caroni's suicide to them, the tomato that explodes against his cheek in juicy fury is the perfect rejection of his hypocrisy. It is not a comic moment. The tomato is more satisfying than the knife—an appropriate nay-saying perfectly aimed and perfectly timed. No wonder Henry Malloran was elected president of the senior class next day.

Jerry Renault is the character from the first book who is the most problematic. Some readers have even argued that he dies from the terrible beating at the end of *The Chocolate War*. In any case, we have worried about him, and of all the characters from the first book we want most of all to know what happened to Jerry. His inclusion in the sequel posed great difficulties for Cormier, as he explained to *Horn Book*: "I suppose the natural thing would have been to bring Jerry back to Trinity and have him confront Archie again. But I didn't want to do that. It would be like rewriting *The Chocolate War*. I wanted to keep him away from Trinity and yet have him involved with a Trinity character. . . . To me he was stubborn and refused to come to life; I worked so hard on him."[6]

The basic problem is that Jerry is inherently passive. His natural instincts are to do nothing. This is why the poster that challenges him to disturb the universe is so fascinating to him. The refusal to sell the chocolates only *seemed* like a heroic action because of the circumstances that led up to it. Actually, once the refusal is set in motion, Jerry's natural inertia keeps it in place. The only uncharacteristic thing he does is to strike out at Emile in the boxing ring, and as soon as he does it he knows it is wrong. That single blow guarantees that he will lose.

It is hard for a novelist to work with such a character. How can passivity be made interesting, or even—as it needed to be in this case—heroic? Cormier experimented in early versions of *Beyond the Chocolate War* with sinking Jerry even deeper into inertia. "I had him mute for a good time. In that version because of the language problem in Canada, he wasn't speaking, and suddenly he realized that he couldn't talk anymore. So when he came back to the States, he wasn't able to communicate at all during Goober's first visit. In fact, because he wasn't able to talk, he let out a terrible scream of frustration that sent The Goober out of his home in horror. I wrote several scenes in which he was trying to talk and was talking haltingly. It just wasn't working for me; it just didn't ring true."[7] Glimpses of this version remain in Jerry's attraction to The Talking Church.

It is necessary for dramatic reasons that Jerry should balance Archie's evil and transcend his own previous defeat. But how to do it without doing violence to the character's basic nature? The triumphant solution comes when Jerry discovers the power to defuse evil with an active commitment to passive resistance. He, with The Goober trailing along, tracks down Emile and confronts him, knowing that he will be beaten again. But this time Jerry wins. "Arms at his sides, looking defenseless but knowing where his strength *was*, where it had to be, he advanced toward Janza." Emile hits and hits, and Jerry absorbs the punishment without ever lifting a fist, until Janza retreats, confused and disappointed. It is the beginning of victory for Jerry.

"He'll probably go back to Trinity and go through a Purgatory but be triumphant in the end even though he looks as if he's defeated," speculates Cormier. "I was very tentative about writing those scenes, and I really had to work hard on them. I didn't want a fourteen-year-old kid to sound like a Christ figure. He still had to sound like a kid. That's why I made him groping, not quite sure what he wanted to do. But he still has a quest, a mission. . . . He may become a contemplative; in a way I tried to hint at that in the first scenes when he was praying in Canada, repairing his mind and body and soul."[8]

So here again is the theme that has given Cormier so much trouble: the young person who is irresistibly drawn to leave the world for religious seclusion. This is the theme that he struggled unsuccessfully to bring to life in the unpublished "In the Midst of Winter," the theme that flawed *Bumblebee* in the shape of Cassie's unmotivated and unexplained attraction to the Hacienda. But here in *Beyond the Chocolate War* it works at last. Jerry is a natural-born contemplative, and it does make sense that he should eventually find solace as "a good and kind brother like Brother Eugene . . . someone to fight the Archie Costellos and even the Brother Leons."

The truly tragic figure, it now becomes apparent, is not Jerry, but The Goober. He has admirable instincts for good—but always too late. "I should have refused," he thinks about his part in causing the collapse of Room Nineteen and Brother Eugene. But he didn't. He should have fought by Jerry's side that terrible night, but he stayed away until the moment was past. He tries to find forgiveness, by confessing his guilt to Jerry and by trying to help fight Emile. But again fate makes him a traitor. When Jerry tries to make him understand how "you can get beat up and still not lose," The Goober doesn't get it. All he knows is that he is dogged by guilt and that he will have to give up his friendship with Jerry rather than continue to betray him. Jerry, too, is planning to spare The Goober by letting the friendship fade away, rather than let him tag along and be hurt by a mission he doesn't understand. But they are each acting out of concern for the other, and after all, they have all summer to talk. Can we hope that Jerry will manage to share some of his salvation with poor old Goob?

Archie, of course, is the most interesting character in the book. The more we know about him the more fascinating he becomes. Although Cormier has shown Archie in scenes that reveal his essence in new ways, he has not yielded to the temptation to humanize him, perhaps by allowing him a weakness or two or an occasional endearing quality. He remains completely evil, utterly cold, aloof, and alone. "I am Archie!" he exults. Other people exist only to be used by him.

In metaphor, Archie is the Pope of Darkness. At the Vigils meeting, when Obie and Carter ceremoniously elevate the box of marbles like a demonic Host, Archie lifts his hands, "palms downward, almost as if he were about to bless the Congregation." Later, he thinks of "the gospel of Trinity as written by Archie Costello." When he offers false sympathy to Obie, he takes his loss "upon himself like a cross." Leon, in his arrogance as headmaster, is emperor to Archie's pope: "he treated the students as if they were underlings, mere subjects in the kingdom of his royal highness, Leon the First." But Archie is no follower to anyone, not even the Prince of Darkness. "Archie recognized no eternity, neither heaven nor hell." The external world is for him a hellish projection of his own internal chaos. As he waits in the twilight for an encounter with Brother Leon, he imagines that the dark is providing places for people to hide. "Archie always envisioned lurkers, predators, watchers in the shadow or around corners, peeking out of windows, waiting behind closed doors. . . . It was a rotten world, full of treachery and evil. . . ."

Archie is above the messiness of human relationships. "I don't hate anybody or anything," he says, truthfully. Only one thing arouses his fury and scorn: goodness. Obie's newfound happiness in his love for Laurie disgusts Archie, and he lashes out venomously at Carter's "honor and pride." Although he is brilliantly, subtly intelligent, real thinking is as repellent to him as emotion. "People thought too much, anyway," he observes. Because evil, as we have said before, is essentially pointless; think it through, and it loses its meaning and power. Archie cannot afford to think.

Neither can he afford to feel. In this book Cormier has finally allowed us to see the sexual dimension of Archie's nature. Unlike the masturbation scene that Cormier edited from *The Chocolate War*, the passage in which Archie has sex with Jill Morton in his car is passionless. He fears the goodness of the body, allowing himself "measures of enjoyment . . . but always holding a part of himself aloof, never letting go completely." Archie cares nothing about Morton, so he can talk to her. "He told her everything. And nothing." Although actually we know that "Miss Jerome's" is a girl's school, Cormier evokes a whorehouse and a loveless encounter between professional and customer. "Archie usually came to Morton, his favorite of all the girls at Miss Jerome's" because of "her willingness to please and her knowing ways." "You haven't been around for a while," she says, like a floozie in an old movie.

Although the coupling of Archie and Morton is cold, it is fairly explicit and definitely erotic. Other scenes in *Beyond the Chocolate War* are also sensual. The passionate explorations of Obie and Laurie, for example, or the "rape." Other young adult books by Cormier have had almost no overt sexual action, so it is interesting that he would choose to write such scenes now in what he has admitted is "a very conservative time." When he sent the completed manuscript to his publisher he worried for a time that someone might ask for cuts; he was pleased when he got full support for the book just as he had written it.[9]

In *Beyond the Chocolate War* Cormier has come into his full strength as a brilliant storyteller, and there is no need for that play with metaphors and allusions for the sheer joy of virtuosity that characterized the style of *The Chocolate War*. But there are many arresting phrases that strike home a meaning like Carter's gavel, "a hammer driving a nail through wood into flesh." Jerry and his father occupy their apartment "the way mannequins inhabit rooms of furniture in a department store." Archie's laugh is "a sound as dry as rolling dice"; his words are "as cold as ice cubes rattling in a tray." When Obie reminds him, with a look, of the chocolates, "something flickered in Archie's eyes, as if an invisible branch had snapped across his face." After Fair Day "the Trinity grounds lay battered and bruised in the fading sunlight. . . . The lawn was trampled and tired, the abandoned booths and tables looming like the skeletons of awkward animals in the dying light." Ray thinks wistfully of "the sea lapping the shore like the tongue of an old and friendly dog."

There are brief references from the Cormier symbology that have become almost obligatory: a menacing dog, a whiff of lilac, a forbidding nun. Names often reveal hidden meanings to the Cormier reader who is willing to dig a bit. A particularly intricate example here is the case of Bunting's two stooges Harley and Cornacchio. The first name brings to mind the hulking menace of a huge motorcycle. *Cornacchia* in Italian is a crow, a rook, a bird of ill-omen, and the second name might be the masculine form of the word. But there is more. "Cornacchio and Harley" sounds like a pair of henchmen from the commedia dell'arte, the medieval theater of Italy that traded on masked stock characters like Harlequin—which might be shortened to "Harley." And even more—the origin of *Harlequin* is from the old French, meaning "leader of a troop of demon horsemen riding at night," which recalls the two of them bushwhacking unwary lovers with an invading spotlight.

Cormier the magician has always entertained his readers with secrets and games, illusions and surprises. In *Beyond the Chocolate War* his bag of magic tricks yields one astonishment after another. Ray Bannister calls misdirection "the magician's most powerful tool," and, as he explains it, "a magician guided the audience to see what the magician wanted them to see, made them think they were seeing one thing while another surprise awaited them." Cormier is a master of this technique. Caroni's oblique references to "the Letter" misdirect us to think of it as a missive like Carter's note to Leon, until it is revealed as a test grade. The realistic tone of the scene in which Leon opens a package lulls us, so that we are astounded when it blows his head off, and jarred again when at the end of the paragraph we realize that it is Caroni's fantasy and we have been fooled. Other illusions of death abound: Leon shot by a sniper, Obie's dream of the guillotine, Ray as a killer in the false newspaper clipping, the near-misses of Caroni's first try at suicide, Leon pricked by his knife—and Obie's murder attempt.

But the illusion of the black marble is Cormier's most amazing and complex effect. Archie has always drawn the white marble, which releases him from responsibility, and we never wondered why. But at the first Vigils meeting his draw is a bit too quick and glib. Remembering Ray's sleight-of-hand practice, we begin to wonder if perhaps Archie's good luck has had some help. Later, Obie is struck with the same insight when he sees Ray make a red ball, "no larger than a marble," vanish and reappear. He remembers that Archie had been presented with the box by surprise only once (at the disastrous boxing match), and on that occasion "sweat had danced on his forehead—Archie, who never perspired—and he had looked apprehensive." We are sure that his discomfiture was because he was not prepared with a sleight. Our suspicions are confirmed when we learn (through the incident of the fake clipping) that he is no stranger to the magic store in Worcester. So we are as startled as Archie is when he draws the black marble from the box that Obie has so carefully rigged to expose his sleight-of-hand. Cormier has misdirected us, and much later we are surprised even again, when Archie tells Obie that he deliberately took the black marble, to find out what would happen, how far Obie would go. But why then was he startled? Mysteries still remain after the trick is completed.

All through both books we have longed for Archie to get the black marble. But when he finally does, Cormier plays one last masterpiece of a trick. He cheats us of the sweetness of retribution by manipulating our sympathies. The delicious first sight of Archie as The Fool is not as delicious as we thought it was going to be. As he is led (the great Archie—led!) across the parking lot, head held high in spite of the "Kick Me" sign on his back, suddenly we very much do *not* want to see him humiliated. When he sits quietly on the platform of the Water Game, "neat and spotless in his chino pants and white jersey," he has dignity, grace, even nobility. The crowd is silent and hangs back. When Obie tries to bribe a boy to throw the ball at the target that will drop Archie, soaked and struggling, into the pool, he protests, "I'm not dunking any Archie Costello." Neither are we. When the hawker dismisses him ("I'd go broke with you there all day long . . .") and he leaps gracefully to the ground, we feel like cheering. It is no surprise when nobody is willing to *kick* any Archie Costello either.

But what about the guillotine? It must fall, but if we didn't want Archie dunked we certainly don't want him beheaded. As he kneels so coolly to be "executed," he has become a heroic figure, and it is Obie who is despicable. The tension at this point is almost unbearable. Cormier has built it to the shrieking point with one emotional scene quickly following another. The audience is in the palm of his hand. The blade descends—but before it reaches its target we are plunged into the midst of Caroni's suicide. Only when his body hits the ground with the "hollow, thudding sound" we expected from the guillotine, only then is the tension released.

The illusion is ended. In the next line Archie marvels "You wanted to kill me, Obie," and we know we have been misdirected again. Archie, of course, did not know that he was about to lose his head. What seemed to be dignity and bravery was only casual acceptance of a silly magic show. The trappings of an execution have made us believe in Archie as the heroic condemned criminal. Now suddenly he is the old Archie and our loathing is firmly back in place as he demolishes Obie by praising him for attempting murder. And then he shows Obie where the guilt really lies for all the evil at Trinity.

But can it be that this is one final piece of misdirection? Obie knows that he could have, should have, refused to follow Archie. But isn't it true that things would have been different if Archie Costello had never registered at Trinity? Obie cries out in anguish, "This could have been a beautiful place to be, Archie. A beautiful time for all of us." If he had said *no*—or if Archie had not been there to require a *no*.

Archie has had it all his way for four years, and now as he leaves Trinity he sets one last scheme in motion that will bring the school down around Brother Leon's ears for good. Cormier has said, "It bothered me that I'd created Bunting to be the Assigner, because he is so unlike Archie. Then it occurred to me that Archie has a motive for picking a kid like Bunting. Archie doesn't want someone there who would outdo him. He really isn't going to tell Bunting his secrets about how to manipulate people."[10] Subtlety goes right over Bunting's head. He is a thug, and an incompetent one at that. Archie is pleased when he botches the rape—"he was delighted because he saw that Bunting was perfect for what he had planned for the future." The plan is diabolical in its simplicity: he saddles Bunting with Emile Janza as right-hand man, and then he offers Emile a number of suggestions about how things might be run next year. Bunting bites the bait gladly—violence is something he understands.

So the book ends as it started—in deepening darkness. Or does it? There *is* hope for next year if you know where to look for it. Henry Malloran with his knack for well-timed action is president; levelheaded Ray Bannister will still be around; Jerry and The Goober may be back with new strength. And doesn't Brother Leon know very well how to squelch the kind of disturbance Bunting and Janza have in mind? Things may work out for Trinity with Archie gone.

Yes, but remember—Archie has now been let loose on the world.

When the critics were let loose on *Beyond the Chocolate War*, they were nearly unanimous in their agreement that it was a worthy sequel. Only Roger Sutton, writing for *School Library Journal*, felt that "readers new to Trinity may be puzzled by what is essentially a string of thematic reverberations. . . . Individually, many scenes are vividly horrific, but as a whole this is less compelling as fiction than it is as a commentary on *The Chocolate War*—Cormier here intensifies and explicates what was powerfully implicit in the first book."[11] Hazel Rochman made a similar comment in the *New York Times Book Review*: "With its complexity, *Beyond the Chocolate War* is not as starkly dramatic as its predecessor. It relies too much on Mr. Cormier's explication, and there is less action and more emphasis on the internal lives of many characters."[12] Yet Rochman's review of the sequel was generally favorable, and other reviewers were enthusiastic.

Sally Estes, in *Booklist*, said "this novel is more complex in construction, style, theme, and characterization than its predecessor—indeed, the portrayal of Archie, in particular is much more finely honed and convincing."[13] Teenager Marcia Cohen spoke for young people in *Seventeen* magazine: "Beautifully crafted characters and a fast-paced, compelling plot make Cormier's novel one to read and remember."[14] Stephanie Nettell of the London *Times Literary Supplement* marveled at its power and called it a "searing, painful book."[15] The *Horn Book*, in a review by Mary M. Burns, was even more unstinting with praise. *Beyond the Chocolate War*, she wrote, is "remarkable for maintaining the balance between plot and philosophy characteristic of the most memorable novels. Quite simply, the work is one of Cormier's finest books to date: combining the sense of immediacy that a good newsman can convey with the psychological insight of a mature writer."[16] And *Voice of Youth Advocates*, in a review by Gayle Keresey, hailed it as "the best of Cormier's highly acclaimed novels" and called for its inclusion on the annual Best Books for Young Adults list of the Young Adult Services Division of the American Library Association.[17]

But this was not to be. Probably owing to the persuasive presence on the selection committee of Sutton and Rochman, *Beyond the Chocolate War* was not named a Best Book—making it the only one of Cormier's young adult novels not to be so honored. This is a small slight when considered in the larger perspective taken by *Horn Book*: "His are among the few books written for young adults which, in all probability, will still be discussed in the twenty-first century."[18]

7. *I Am the Cheese*

TAPE YAK 001 0213 date deleted P-R

P: Stop.

R: You mean stop reading?

P: Yes. You, the reader. Right here. First, before you go on, you must answer one question.

R: What do you want to know?

P: Have you read *I Am the Cheese* yet?

R: No. I thought I'd read this chapter first.

P: That would be a great pity. It would spoil things for you—the suspense, the intriguing perplexities, the myriad shocks of discovery, the false leads—in a word, the fun. I would emphatically advise that you make the journey with Adam before you cover the same ground a second time with me.

R: All right.

P: Excellent. We shall continue afterwards. Let us suspend now.

END TAPE YAK 001

And so, having finished the book, the reader is irresistibly compelled to turn back to the beginning and, like Adam, begin all over again. The story circles back on itself, revolving like the wheels of a bicycle, like children in a ring playing "The Farmer in the Dell." But for the reader, unlike Adam, each time the experience is different.

The first time through, we know only what Adam knows. Our blank spaces are his, and the truth comes to us—and to him—in a series of disorienting jolts. As the *New York Times* said, "the book is assembled in mosaic fashion: a tiny chip here, a chip there, and suddenly the outline of a face dimly begins to take shape. Everything is related to something else. . . ."[1] But this is far too simple a description. Perry Nodelman, in his incisive article "Robert Cormier Does a Number," has attempted to analyze the complex and unsettling experience of a first reading of *I Am the Cheese*.

A reader's first impulse, Nodelman observes, is to approach the story as a logical, detached detective. The key, it seems, is in understanding the events of the mysterious past. But this leads to anxiety, disorientation, and confusion—"that uncertainty we call suspense"—because the events of the present are not clear. "Since we do not know what effects the mysterious past we are trying to understand led to, we act less with the cool certainty of mystery novel detectives than with the anxiety of confused people asked to think logically about incomplete information. That sounds uncomfortable—and it is. Cormier cleverly makes us accept and enjoy our confusion by providing *one* genuine past . . . and what appear to be *two* different presents that that past led to. . . . With our attention focused on sorting such things out, looking for clues and making guesses, we accept our uncertainty about present circumstances as part of the pleasure of the mystery."

The one possibility that never occurs to us, continues Nodelman, is that both presents are happening at once, that Adam is at the same time on a journey to Rutterburg and being interrogated by Brint. "Cormier cannot allow us to consider it, for it depends on our knowledge that the bike trip is a fantasy, knowledge that is the key to the entire mystery. He deflects our attention from the literal truth of the novel, the impeccably chronological ordering of events that seem to have no chronology, by making them seem to have no chronology. How Cormier manipulates readers into believing the wrong things and ignoring the right ones is fascinating to explore."[2]

A close look at the two opening chapters, first as a novice and then as an experienced reader of *I Am the Cheese*, will illustrate this process. In the beginning we know only that someone is riding a bicycle from Monument to Rutterburg. Who? Why? A young person, evidently, who has been close enough to his father still to want to use an old bike like his, even though it makes him pedal "furiously"—a strangely intense word. The rhythm of the paragraph suggests the steady pumping of his legs. Then the first tiny hint of something sinister: "the wind like a snake slithering up my sleeves."

In the second paragraph we learn that the sight of a hospital reminds the rider of his father in Rutterburg. Is he ill there? Is the journey to visit him? Whatever it is, it must be urgent because the cyclist accelerates his pedaling at the thought. Then another hint of chill—the rotten October. The love of Thomas Wolfe that the cyclist has shared with his father confirms our guess about their relationship, and the elderly phrase used to describe a teacher—"he regarded me with suspicion"—tells us that the person is a student, young but bookish and probably solitary. And he is kind—he waves when he passes a child who looks lonesome. But why does he think someone might be following him? Now he tells us he didn't wave good-bye to anybody when he left on this trip. Why not? Where were they? This is not the kind of person who skips school and goes away without at least telling someone. It doesn't fit. We begin to feel puzzled.

Immediately, Cormier gives us what seems to be an explanation of sorts: the irrational fears, and later, the pills, tell us that the bike rider has emotional problems. But why? Other questions come fast now. What is the gift? Why are his father's clothes in the cellar? If he has money, why doesn't he take the bus?—his reasons ring a bit hollow. Why is it so important that he go on his own power? And why must he do it this way "for his father"? The intensity of his determination seems inappropriate—but perhaps it is a sign of his unbalanced state.

Then another character is introduced: Amy Hertz. She, we know immediately, is a very different kind of person. "What the hell, as Amy says, philosophically." A tough, cocky, self-assured sort of person. The fact that such a girl is the object of the bike rider's love tells us more about his needs (and also confirms that he is a young *man*). But his reasons for not phoning her before he leaves seem logical. When he dumps his pills into the garbage disposal he seems "reckless and courageous" to us as well as to himself, and when a car howls its horn at him "for straying too far into the roadway" we think it is a result of that recklessness. It becomes apparent that the journey is going to be long and grueling, and as the boy struggles through, breaks free, and is off on his way, we are too busy exulting with him to notice that we have been left with a double handful of unanswered questions.

The second chapter clarifies nothing; indeed, it adds a second layer of perplexities. The preceding chapter was in the present tense, and so is this one, at first. Has the boy been in some sort of an accident that has put him here in the hands of a doctor? Or is this even the same boy? Is one of the chapters a flashback to the other? Which? The form is even more puzzling. It seems to be some sort of official record of a tape recording, but for what possible reason can the date have been deleted? Why is the questioner labeled "T" when his name is Brint? Does it stand for "tape"? Or "therapist," perhaps? (Cormier himself has said that he used "T" because it is the *last* letter of Brint's name[3]—but, then, can that statement be part of the Number?) Even for a psychiatrist his speech is strangely stilted and formal: "shall," "I have been advised," and that ominous phrase from the torture chamber, "the better it will be for you." But when the questioning turns to the boy's earliest memories we are on familiar ground again. Isn't that how people always begin with a therapist? Even the sense of menaced flight that pervades the boy's story could be explained by his mental illness, as could his perception of Brint as threatening. Except for two disquieting details: the cigarettes that his father never again smoked, and the way Brint pounces on the word *clues*. When the boy dissolves in panic, almost, but not quite, we believe in Brint's benevolence when he says, "Everything's going to be all right." But there have been no answers to some basic questions, nor will there be any until many, many pages later. As Nodelman says, "novelists usually make us ask such questions at the beginnings of novels, in order to arouse our interest. But they usually quickly answer them, and then focus our attention on new developments. . . . In keeping us in the dark . . . Cormier extends throughout most of *I Am the Cheese* the disorientation we usually stop feeling a short way into other novels."

"A second reading . . . is a different experience. Now the novel seems filled with clues, with obvious evidence of what seemed incomprehensible before, and with huge ironies."[4] All of Adam's forgotten past is still available to us, and we can see his buried knowledge at work on the fabric of his fantasy. As he goes about his preparations for the journey to Rutterburg, we also at the same time see him preparing for the ride around the hospital grounds, and we know that the road he will travel in his imagination is the same route he and his parents took on the fatal "vacation" trip, in a different Thomas Wolfe October. This time we know why he doesn't wave good-bye to anyone and why he talks himself out of calling Amy. It is his own loneliness that stands on the sidewalk in the form of a child and his own fear of Them that follows behind invisibly. His fear needs a face, so he tells himself that he is afraid of elevators, exposed open spaces, rooms without windows, dogs—all animals, in fact, plus snakes and spiders ("they are not rational," he explains later, cryptically). He knows there is good reason for terror, but he dare not give it its true name.

Even though he has money, he must talk himself into pedaling the bike because he is going nowhere there are buses, and he "travels light" because he needs no "provisions or extra clothing" for that trip inside the fence. His father's jacket and cap are, to him, in the basement because that is where he last saw them in his past, even though Dr. Dupont has brought them to him here in the hospital. And Pokey the Pig, who represents the safe comfort of childhood and will be gift-wrapped, is in "the cabinet in the den" where Adam searched for and found the first terrible evidence of his own nonexistence. He dresses in his father's clothes and looks in the mirror as if to bring him back to life. But he must justify it to his conscious mind by remarking how good the cap is for the cold. It is the hospital that has provided him with the mind-clouding green and black capsules that he pours into the sink. And it is the memory of the car that killed his mother that blares past as he leaves the driveway. Only his thoughts of Amy are fresh and clear and not overlaid with anything else.

Now when Adam tells Brint the story of his parents' escape we know why "their voices scratched at the night," why Adam's father never smoked again, why there were purple half-moons under his mother's eyes. The slightly inappropriate word *clues* has, of course, been implanted in his mind by Brint during earlier investigations. When Adam says, "It's as if I was born that night," we appreciate the irony, and when he wants to tell Pokey how brave and clever he has been, we recall with poignance that in the end—and now—there is no one *but* Pokey to listen sympathetically to such confidences. Even the number of the tape—OZK001—is significant. It reminds us of *The Wizard of Oz* and Dorothy's return to Kansas where she, like Adam, is reunited with the real people who appear as fantasy characters in her dream.[5] But Cormier is still not through playing games with us. Adam associates the lilac perfume with his mother—but in the last chapter of the book he has noticed that fragrance in the hallway of the hospital. And we still don't really know why Brint is recorded as "T."

The triple strands that are braided together to make the story, the three alternating levels on which the narrative progresses, are an intricate but internally consistent device. The bike ride is told in first-person present tense. The tapes, as dialogue, have neither person nor tense (but we assume they are happening in the present), and the revelation of Adam's past that grows out of the tapes proceeds chronologically and is in third-person past tense. A slightly confusing factor is that in the early phases of the bike ride Adam enjoys some memories of the warm, safe times of his childhood—and these fit into the chronology of the memories he is sharing with Brint. This is all perfectly clean-cut and clear the second time around, but a first-time reader feels that the events of the story have been scrambled intriguingly.

Of all the sinister characters Cormier has created to embody his ideas about evil, Brint is perhaps the most chilling. Indeed, it is tempting at first to jump to the conclusion, because of his stiffly formal speech, that he is a machine, perhaps some kind of interrogation computer. Tempting, because the worst thing about Brint, the most appalling realization, is that he *is* (or *was*) a human being, but he has been so corrupted by his immersion in evil that he can sit year after year across from Adam, calmly herding him through lacerating self-discoveries and feeling not one flicker of pity or mercy. Only twice does he seem human, but in both cases it is immediately clear that the pose is a trick. At one point he exclaims about the beauty of the weather—but only to jolly Adam out of a deep withdrawal. Later, when Adam is remembering his father's distrust of Grey, he suddenly sees something in Brint's expression that makes him suspect that he is "one of those men who had been his father's enemy." Brint, realizing that he has almost given himself away, covers quickly. "I am sorry that you were disturbed by the expression on my face. I, too, am human. I have headaches, upset stomach at times. I slept badly last night. Perhaps that's what you saw reflected on my face." But Adam is not entirely convinced. "It's good to find out you're human," he grants uncertainly. "Sometimes I doubt it."

Much of the content of the dialogue portion of the tapes is the progress of Adam's reluctant realization that Brint is his enemy. He wants so much to believe in him as a benevolent father-figure, who has his welfare at heart, that sometimes he even tries to prompt Brint into this role. He wonders aloud why Brint never asks him about his mother, and another time he is a bit hurt when Brint interrupts his reminiscences, and he says plaintively, "You sound impatient. I'm sorry. Am I going into too much detail? I thought you wanted me to discover everything about myself." Later he finally cannot avoid noticing that it is only certain kinds of information that interest his interrogator, although he repeatedly protests that he has only Adam's welfare at heart. But Adam really does know the truth about Brint, and he cannot entirely hide it from himself, even at the beginning. In the second tape he says, "He had a kindly face although sometimes his eyes were strange. The eyes stared at him occasionally as if the doctor—if that's what he was—were looking down the barrel of a gun, taking aim at him. He felt like a target." Adam is completely in Brint's power, both physically and mentally. The windows of the interrogation room are barred; the shots and the pills control his feelings and his mind. To recognize his captor as the enemy is unbearable, and so he pushes away the knowledge as long as he can and tries to find goodness in Brint. And so does the reader. It is this blurring of the distinction between good and evil that gives the tapes their peculiar horror, and that points to the larger theme of the book.

Cormier has had some revealing things to say about Brint. He chose the name, he says, to suggest someone bloodless and cold, to rhyme with *flint* and *glint*.[6] At first he was not sure whether the character was a psychiatrist or not. "But I thought this would be the way it would sound if a character were using a slight knowledge of psychology to take advantage of a situation."[7] Brint's knowledge may be "slight," but he has certainly learned the superficial tricks of the trade, as when he turns Adam's suspicions back on himself by accusing him of attacking his therapist to create a diversion whenever certain buried information is approached. In the Brint/Adam interchange there is a hint of a theme that Cormier was to explore more thoroughly in *After the First Death*: "Adam comes to him completely innocent in his amnesia, and Brint corrupts that. That's what evil is, the destruction of innocence." Although Cormier emphasizes Brint's machinelike quality by never giving us any description or background, he claims he has a home life in mind for him. "I picture Brint in a two-car garage, a family, belongs to the Elks. . . . He has this job in an agency where he's got to keep questioning all these people, but at night he leaves the area and goes home and has a regular life. . . ." Somehow the idea of Brint presiding over a suburban household seems like part of the Number. Has Cormier forgotten that Brint is instantly available to Adam in the night? Obviously he sleeps nearby in the hospital, probably in a spartan room where he hangs his impeccable suit neatly in the closet. Then he lies rigidly on a narrow cot all night without rumpling the covers, stretched out on his back with folded arms. He does not allow himself to dream.

At a crucial point in the narrative, Brint lays out some priorities. "Permit me to summarize. The first landmark was that day in the woods with the dog. The second landmark was that call from Amy." The Dog, as both symbol and event, recurs often in Adam's narrative. In the first chapter, the very thought of "all the dogs that would attack me on the way to Rutterburg, Vermont," almost keeps him from setting out on the journey. He keeps an eye out for dogs when he does get on the road, and sure enough, soon he is threatened by one. As soon as we know that the bike trip is unreal, it is clear that this is a dream dog. The breed is German shepherd, a kind of animal associated with official power, police, Nazis. He is black, and, like Brint, he looks at Adam silently "with eyes like marbles." And, contrary to the normal behavior of dogs, he is guarding an empty house where there is no owner to defend. As in a dream, the direct attack is deflected to the tires. The beast tries "to topple the bike, send it askew and have me crashing to the roadway, his victim," just as Brint with his persistent questions tries to topple the delicate structure of defense that allows Adam to delude himself with the imaginary escape of the trip to Rutterburg. Even when Adam has eluded this animal, he has a prophetic feeling "that the dog will pursue me forever."

In the tape immediately following, Adam offers a startling remark. "Maybe the dog is a clue," he says tentatively. It sounds as if he is referring to the dog he has just escaped in the preceding chapter. Is this a link finally between the two separate narrative streams? But the idea is aborted as soon as Adam clarifies his statement: "I thought of the dog when I looked out this morning and saw a dog on the grass." Brint assumes that he is talking about Silver, the dog that experienced readers know is kept on the hospital grounds, and that Adam has been wary of as he returned to reality from the end of his trip. But Silver is the third dog evoked in this conversation, not the second. The dog Adam is recalling is the animal that attacked his father in the woods, a dog that first-time readers have not yet met, except through Adam's fears. Here Cormier achieves an extraordinary effect. The question of which dog is reflection and which dog is real becomes multiplied and confused, and the image is of dogs, single and several, reflected endlessly in a trick mirror. This moment plants a subliminal suggestion that the three strands of narrative are one story, returning to the now double meaning of Adam's casual "Maybe the dog is a clue."

The dog in the woods is, of course, the central dog. This episode has a surreal tone, although it is part of the memories retrieved by Brint's questioning, and therefore true. The battle of the father and the dog is unnecessary to the story line, strictly speaking, but as a metaphor it is a compelling side-trip for Cormier. The key is Adam's description of the growling dog: "the way it stood there, implacable, blocking their path. There was something threatening about the dog, a sense that the rules didn't apply, like encountering a crazy person and realizing that anything could happen, anything was possible." Implacable, no appeal, like the forces that have trapped Adam—and in memory he savors his father's courage in battle and his victory.

And finally, it is a dog that brings the whole complex narrative structure down to one focus. As Adam returns sadly and quietly from his long trip, he wheels through the grounds of "the hospital" and is met by a kindly doctor. Has he at last broken free and come to a safe place? But as soon as he meets Silver in the hall, the momentary hope is blasted. We have seen Silver before, through the window of Brint's office, and we know now without a doubt that Adam has never left the place of interrogation.

Brint's second landmark is the call from Amy. The reader, like Brint, suspects that there was more to this incident than met Adam's ear. "Was Amy part of the conspiracy?" is a frequent question in Cormier's mail. The letter writers wonder shrewdly if she was prompted by the enemy to probe Adam's past, or if perhaps the name "Hertz" is meant to suggest that she "hurts" him. This Cormier denies emphatically. Amy is innocent and, as Adam wished, quite separate from the structure of intrigue, and the reason she is no longer there after three years is not that the enemy got her, but simply that her family moved away. Actually, Amy is the opposite of hurtful to Adam. She, as he says, "brought brightness and gaiety to his life." Cormier introduced her out of compassion for his protagonist: "I was conscious that Adam was leading a very drab life—his father a shadow, his mother withdrawn, and he was introverted—and I thought, this is getting pretty dull. So I introduced her to liven up the book, to give him a little love and affection, and, of course, instantly I fell in love with her." As Cormier's female characters often do, Amy led her creator pages and pages out of the way into episodes that had to be discarded later.

Amy, with her quick imagination, her antic sense of humor, her tender toughness and her nonchalance, is truly a charming creation. But what lies behind that toughness? Does her mother's preoccupation with committee work have something to do with it? We see her only through Adam's adoring eyes, but actually all is not well with Amy's soul. Amy, like Adam, is an outsider, a loner. Her Numbers have more than a little anger in them; they are not funny to the victims. Sometimes they have a strained quality, like the caper in the church parking lot, or depend for their effect on an enigmatic quirk of thought, like the cartful of baby-food jars left in front of the Kotex display in the supermarket. She really needs Adam to laugh with her. There is nobody else in the audience.

To Adam, the Numbers are "heady and hilarious but somehow terrible." To defy authority is foreign to his nature. But through his participation in the Numbers he gains the courage to investigate the mysteries about his past. "I, too, am capable of mischief," he thinks as he eavesdrops on his father and Mr. Grey. Thoughts of Amy give him courage on the bike ride, too. "What the hell, as Amy would say," he tells himself. Her last real words to Adam are a casual "Call me," and throughout his eternal bike rides he tries. Or thinks he tries. He makes excuses, or he calls at the wrong time, or he hangs up because the wise guys are approaching. He really knows that after three years Amy Hertz has disappeared from his life, and there is no comfort to be found at 537–3331. When he does finally make the connection with that number the Number is over, and it is the beginning of the end of his illusion.

Adam is to some extent based on Cormier himself as a boy. Not only his fears and phobias and migraines, but his personality and ambitions recall Cormier at fourteen. He is shy and book-loving, and home is a warm, safe retreat from a hostile world where wise guys lie in wait at every corner. Like Jerry in *The Chocolate War*, he knows only too well the scenario that begins "You lookin' for trouble?" Cormier betrayed in the operating room is vividly evoked when Adam says, "I don't like to be confined or held down. My instinct, then, is to get up on my feet, flailing my arms at anything that might try to hold me down, confine me." When Adam explains the writer inherent in his attitude toward life, it is also the young Cormier speaking: "Anyway, his terrible shyness, his inability to feel at ease with people, had nothing to do with his mother. He felt it was his basic character; he preferred reading a book or listening to old jazz records in his bedroom than going to dances or hanging around downtown with the other kids. Even in the fourth or fifth grade, he had stayed on the outskirts of the schoolyard watching the other kids playing the games—Kick the Can was a big thing in the fourth grade—anyway, he had never felt left out: it was his choice. To be a witness, to observe, to let the events be recorded within himself on some personal film in some secret compartment no one knew about, except him. It was only later, in the eighth grade, when he knew irrevocably that he wanted to be a writer, that he realized he had stored up all his observations, all his emotions, for that purpose." And there is poignance for Cormier in the closeness and deep affection Adam feels for his parents, especially the warm glow of love at the last supper at the Red Mill—just before his father's death.

Between creator and creation there is an ironic contrast in one respect. "I'm not built for subterfuge and deception," says Adam. It is this quality that makes him a too-perfect subject for interrogation. Because he is so guileless, they—who are so complex in evil that they cannot comprehend simple honesty—persist in thinking he must be hiding something. Again and again he willingly turns the pockets of his mind inside out for them, but they still suspect he has something up his sleeve. It occurs to him to hold back, but he always ends by telling all.

His resistance has been channeled in other directions. The fantasy bike ride is Adam's gesture of defiance in the face of the Implacable. This explains the fierce intensity of his determination to make the journey "for my father," and the inevitability he feels in the beginning about his decision to go—"I knew I would go the way you know a stone will drop to the ground if you release it from your hand." Like Jerry, his gesture is stubborn and half-aware, not the grand, controlled action of a hero. "I am a coward, really," he admits, but in the refrain "I keep pedaling" there is persistent courage. Adam must repeatedly overcome obstacles and break through his fears, but each time he does he can soar for a moment and he finds new hope and strength.

As in dreams real emotions are translated into fantasy people and events, so as the bike ride progresses Adam's hidden awareness of the menace all around him begins to come to the forefront of his mind and take on personification, shape, and form as Whipper and the wise guys, as Fat Arthur and Junior Varney, as snarling dogs and the terrible ferocious vomit-pink car with the grinning grille. Meanwhile in the interrogations he is bringing to consciousness memories that bleed their terror into his secret life of the mind so that he is less and less able to sustain the fantasy. As he approaches the final truth, his newly discovered knowledge of the amount of time that has passed intrudes into the dream in a collision of logics. When he gets to the motel where he and his parents spent a safe night "last summer" he finds it "feels as if it has been neglected for years and years." The effect is eerily disorienting. One last time he tries to call Amy, but the gruff man on the phone and his own mind tell him she is gone; he is no longer able to delude himself with hopes of her comfort or with the defiant illusion of escape. He wants to wake up—"I would give anything to be folded into bed, the pills working their magic, soothing me"—and in a moment he does. The dream begins to smear and waver like the woman's face through the wet windshield. Everything slows down; sounds are distorted, like a movie in a disintegrating projector. The darkness gathers him. Yet still—on a first reading—still we believe this is reality.

Like Amy, Cormier "always withholds information about the Numbers until the last possible moment, stretching out the drama." Even here at the end, there is one last tiny gleam of false hope. We think Adam has arrived in Rutterburg at last. Then he turns the corner and sees the hospital, and as he greets one by one the people from his fantasy the shattering truth crashes down. For the first time he sings the *last* verse of "The Farmer in the Dell." The cheese stands alone, and he is the cheese.

The final tape, with its cold, bureaucratic verdict, has been the subject of much speculation. With a little study, a key can be puzzled out:

Subject A—Adam

Personnel #2222—Thompson, or Grey

File Data 865-01—the record of Adam's father's testimony and subsequent official events related to it

OZK Series—the interrogation tapes between Adam and Brint

Department 1-R—the government agency to which Adam's father testified

Tape Series ORT, UDW—the tapes of Adam's two previous interrogations

Witness #559-6—Adam's father

Policy 979—a rule that "does not currently allow termination procedures by Department 1-R"

And Department 1-R, notice, is the agency to whom Adam's father gave his witness, presumably the good guys, but it is *they* who have imprisoned Adam, and they who are being asked to "obliterate" him. Who, then, are the Adversaries? And Grey? Up to now, it has seemed that it was Grey's legs that Adam saw as he lay on the ground after the crash, but was that just because that person wore gray pants? And Grey, remember, did not "necessarily" wear gray clothes.

Even Cormier's own words from the answer sheet he mails to questioners do not completely clear up the ambiguity: "Grey was not part of the syndicate. He was not a double agent in the usual sense, although he double-crossed Adam's father, setting him up for the syndicate and the accident. He was present at the scene to clean up afterward, but hadn't counted on Adam's survival—an embarrassment to the agency."[8] So whose side is he on? In terms of Adam's future, it matters not at all. As Anne MacLeod puts it, "the two systems are equally impersonal, and equally dangerous to the human being caught between them. What matters to the organization—*either* organization—is its own survival, not Adam's."[9] In the third chapter the old man at the gas station has asked Adam, "Do you know who the bad guys are?" He doesn't, and neither do we. What is so overwhelming here is not just that evil is powerful, but that the good guys and the bad guys turn out to be—probably—indistinguishable. It is not a matter of good against evil, but of the cheese standing alone against everything, his whole world revealed at last as evil. Where now is Cormier's imperative for collective good? There is nobody left to come to his rescue. This is not a metaphor. MacLeod says, "This stark tale comments directly on the real world of government, organized crime, large-scale bureaucracy, the apparatus of control, secrecy, betrayal, and all the other commonplaces of contemporary political life."[10] We could all be the cheese.

"A magnificent accomplishment," said *Hornbook*.[11] "Beside it, most books for the young seem as insubstantial as candyfloss," said the *Times Literary Supplement*.[12] "The secret, revealed at the end, explodes like an H-bomb," said *Publishers Weekly*.[13] "A masterpiece," said *West Coast Review of Books*.[14] The *New York Times Book Review* and the Young Adult Services Division of the American Library Association both included it on their respective lists of best books of the year for young people. But Newgate Callendar wondered in the *New York Times* if the book might turn out to be "above the heads of most teen-agers."[15] Cormier, too, was afraid that he was in danger of losing his newfound young adult audience.[16]

The book had begun as a time-filler. "Sometimes when there's nothing that's compelling, I do exercises. So I put a boy on a bike and had him take off on a Wednesday morning with a box on his bike. Then right away I wondered, what's he doing out of school on a Wednesday morning, where's he going, what's in the package? . . . I started to give him a lot of my own fears, phobias. . . . And I wrote virtually all of the bike part without knowing where it was going."[17] For a while he searched for a second level among religious themes of pilgrimage, the Stations of the Cross, death and resurrection. Then one day, "across my desk at the newspaper . . . came this thing about the Witness Relocation Program. This was at a time when very little was known about it." He began to wonder about the hardships of giving up a past, and "then it struck me, . . . how much harder for a teen, who doesn't even know who he is yet!" He knew he had found his second level. He went back to the bike ride to make it fit.[18] The creation of *I Am the Cheese* was a very intense experience for him. "During the time I was writing the book, no one saw any part of it. I felt like the mad doctor in a laboratory, because I didn't think it would ever work, yet I felt compelled to write it. It was coming out at breakneck speed."[19] "I still picture Adam riding that bike around the institution grounds, as real now as the day I discovered him."[20]

To those who wonder if there have been political repercussions Cormier says, "I know it's critical of government, yet I think the strength of our government is that you *can* be critical of it, because there are so many good things about it, like the very fact that I can write this book."[21] "Believe me, if we did not have a good government, I might have been jailed or my book censored before it ever hit the stores."[22]

Or perhaps the CIA and the Mafia don't read young adult literature.

8. *After the First Death*

"Miro's assignment was to kill the driver. Without hesitation." It is to be his "first death," an eagerly awaited ritual terrorist murder that will mark his transition to manhood and full acceptance into the brotherhood of "freedom fighters." Artkin, the leader of their small band of fanatics, has planned the operation scrupulously. The theater he has chosen for their terrorist act is a school bus full of little children, which unexpectedly turns out, much to Miro's consternation, to be driven this morning by blonde cheerleader Kate Forrester. The terrorists drug the children and force Kate to drive the bus onto an abandoned bridge, where they announce their intentions to the world and the drama begins.

They demand $10 million for their cause, the release of all political prisoners, and the dismantling of Inner Delta, a secret counterterrorist organization at nearby Fort Delta. For every one of their number who is killed, they will kill a child. Meantime, these events are overlaid and interwoven with what seems to be the journal of young Ben Marchand, whose father, General Marcus Marchand, is the secret high command of Inner Delta. Inside the hot, claustrophobic confines of the bus, the tension-filled waiting goes on. One of the children dies from an overdose of the drug in the candy they have been given by Artkin. Afraid of the effect on his plans of another such accident, he gives Kate a temporary stay of execution so that she can keep the children quiet.

Miro is disturbed at losing his victim, and at the same time intrigued by the sexual attraction he is feeling for her. Kate tries to forget her own fears by caring for the children, but is aware of Miro's attraction and attempts to use it to her advantage by making conversation with him. As he tells her about his childhood, his terrorist training, the violence he has been part of in the name of a homeland he has never seen, she realizes that he is without human feeling, "a monster," and that her efforts are pointless. Her horror is intensified when, to convince the watching world that they are serious in their demands, Artkin makes a display of showing the dead child outside on the bridge.

But later she finds a gleam of hope. Kate has a weak bladder under stress, and while changing her damp panties in the back of the bus she discovers an extra ignition key in her wallet. Also she has noticed that one of the children, bright-eyed and chubby Raymond, has not been eating the candy and so is alert but faking sleep, and could be an ally in an escape attempt. Although this last hope is blasted when Artkin discovers Raymond's ruse and forces him to eat the drugged candy, she still has the key. After careful planning and mental rehearsal she makes a desperate try to back the bus off the bridge and succeeds until the engine stalls. Artkin blames Miro, and reprimands him severely.

Now night comes, and the two young people are awake in the dark bus. Miro is puzzled that he is beginning to have emotions: sadness and hate. Kate senses his new vulnerability and tries again to reach him. When she touches his arm he is deeply moved and confused.

Suddenly one of the terrorists is shot by an overanxious sniper, and in retaliation Artkin decides to make Raymond a sacrificial victim, a plan he carries out in spite of Kate's wild offer to take the child's place.

Simultaneously these events have been told a second time from the viewpoint of General Marchand, as his son Ben recalls in his journal the day of the hijacking, when his father summoned him officially to his office. The journal comes to an end, and the general continues. Ben is missing from the room. Where has he gone? The general suspects that he has gone to a nearby bridge to kill himself in remorse. He remembers how he and the terrorists agreed on Ben as a suitably innocent messenger to deliver a stone that would prove to the hijackers that their world leader had been captured. But in the bus Artkin tortures Ben, as his father had known would happen, and Ben reveals what he has learned by accident—the time of a planned attack.

The attack comes, but an hour earlier than the terrorists expect. Artkin is killed, and Miro escapes with Kate as hostage. As they are squeezed together in a hiding place, she taunts him with a sudden realization that Artkin must have been his father. Miro, convulsed in an agony of self-blame for Artkin's death, pulls the trigger of his gun and kills her inadvertently. In a final dialogue between Ben and his father, it is revealed that the general knew from behavorial tests that his son would break under torture, and so sent him to the bridge with deliberately false information to reveal. Unable to live with the knowledge that his father expected him to be a coward and that the whole world knows it, Ben has killed himself, but now returns to take over the guilt-haunted mind of his father. When last seen, Miro, rejecting everything he has learned from his encounter with Kate, is about to strangle a passing motorist and escape to the world at large.

While the construction of *After the First Death* is not as intricate as the circular triple levels of *I Am the Cheese*, it is still a fairly complex structure with built-in puzzles and trapdoors. There are two main narrative streams: the first-person ruminations that are presumably the voice of Ben and later the general, and the events on the bus told in the third person from the alternating perspective of Miro and Kate (and—very briefly—Raymond and one other child).

The first level takes place two weeks before Christmas at (maybe) Castleton Academy, in Pompey, New Hampshire, where Ben has been sent after the summer of the Bus and the Bridge, and (at first reading) seems to last for the space of one afternoon, while Ben types the journal and later his father reads it and waits for him. In the course of these sections the story of the hijacking proceeds in their memory at the same pace as it is being told in the main narrative.

The second level, or Kate-Miro narrative, takes up three times as many pages as the Ben-general sections and is the main device for telling the story. It takes place near Fort Delta and just outside Hallowell, Massachusetts. We know Monument is somewhere close off-stage because the bridge spans Moosock River—a waterway that Adam and Jerry know as Moosock Creek. The action lasts for twenty-four hours—from one morning until the next, with the exception of the introductory scene in which Artkin befuddles a waitress in a café for Miro's benefit. The season is summer, the summer before the time of the Ben-general sections.

In several cases, pieces of action are presented twice, once from the point of view of the participants in the bus, and once from the point of view of the opposition command post. This gives the advantage of expanded perspective and lightens what would otherwise be a story stalled in a very static, claustrophobic situation. It also serves to emphasize parallels between the characters, as when Artkin tells Miro of the terrorist demands and later the general tells Ben the same information.

Perhaps the most difficult element in the book, and one that remains somewhat enigmatic even after close study, is the identity of the voice in the primary narrative, the sections that take place at Castleton Academy. There are two possible interpretations. The first is that Ben sat in his room at the school typing to fill the time before his father was to arrive for a first visit since the hijacking. The general came, was uneasy, and left for a few minutes to recover his composure. Ben typed his feelings about this, then went out to leap off Brimmler's Bridge to his death. His father came back, found the pages, guessed what had happened, and tried to stop Ben but was too late. The shock and guilt unhinged his mind, and in the last section he is in a mental hospital going over and over his need for forgiveness, which compels him to re-create Ben in his own mind and even to give up his identity to him.

A second interpretation, and one that can be substantiated with much internal evidence, is that *all* of these ruminations are the voice of General Marchand, and that we never actually hear Ben. The typing is done by the father in his false identity as the son, and the place is not Castleton Academy but a mental hospital. The general imagines his old school because it is a place where he was happy and where he can easily picture himself as the same age as his son. There are multiple clues to this interpretation. Most obvious is the mother's "Freudian" slip when she calls "Ben" by his father's name—"Mark." (But this clue loses credence a page later when she calls him back from drifting away mentally: " 'Ben,' she said, her voice like the snapping of a tree branch.") When Ben/Mark quotes a teacher's description of the father, the mother points out, "You realize you were describing yourself, don't you?" Ben/Mark does describe himself, but as "a skeleton rattling my bones, a ghost laughing hollow up the sleeves of my shroud, a scarecrow whose straw is soaked with blood." He refers often to being invisible, or to a feeling that someone is listening, looking over his shoulder. At the typewriter he says, "I am a fake, here" and "I am trying to deceive myself not anyone else." The son, seeing his father approaching, finds with terror that his face is a blank, and after the visit types, "It's hard to believe he was really here." About his own death and burial, "Ben" says: "Once in the ground, in the military cemetery at Fort Delta. And again inside of you. Buried me deep inside of you." And toward the end he says, "Put yourself in my place. Or put myself in your place."

It is plain that this is the version that Cormier intends us to accept, even though it is far more difficult and far less satisfying. It is clever and yet somehow not convincing; it feels as if the clues have been scattered in among the lines like so many crumbs for gullible pigeons and English teachers. And there is even a third possibility: could this be entirely Ben's voice, a Ben deluded by his guilt and shame into believing that he can become his forgiving father? A father who has perhaps ended his own guilt by jumping off Brimmler's Bridge? In any one of the three interpretations we miss the perfect click of recognition as the piece fits exactly into place—a click that we learned to love in *I Am the Cheese*.

Other structural devices enrich the deeper meaning of the novel. As in *Wuthering Heights*, each of the main characters can be seen as a reflection of one of the others, a pairing that brings out similarities and contrasts. Miro recognizes this relationship on his first sight of Ben, "the boy who was almost a mirror to himself." They are two sons, two innocents. Artkin and the general are a pair: both fanatical patriots and both fathers willing to sacrifice their sons. There are even two bridges.

Another kind of doubling is the paradoxes that give impact to the themes: murder as virtue, betrayal as service, treachery as patriotism, and above all, innocence as evil. Even the link between Miro and Kate is paradoxical: two young people, sexually attracted to each other and potential lovers but also potential murderer and victim. As *Boston* magazine said, "everybody is either killer or target or both."[1]

After the First Death gives Cormier a chance to show off his powers as a stylist. The book is written in two distinct flavors, which are most strikingly contrasted at the point where the reader first encounters the difference, the switch from part 1 to part 2. Ben's narration has been wavering, limping, truncated paragraphs jumping suddenly from one subject to another. With the introduction of Miro's point of view in part 2 the style changes abruptly and becomes strong and taut and purposeful. There are some brilliant set pieces. Artkin's baiting the waitress is a subtle delight in a book otherwise devoid of joyful moments. In the long paragraph that ends part 8, in which Kate tries to deny to herself that Raymond has been shot, the words skitter frantically like squirrels in a maze with no exit. Artkin's dance of death as he whirls the body of the murdered child above his head like a priest of evil offering a hideous sacrament is an unforgettable evocation of the Black Mass.

The title itself is also part of Cormier's riddling technique. The quotation "After the first death, there is no other" is drawn from the Dylan Thomas poem "A Refusal to Mourn the Death by Fire of a Child in London." It applies in one way or another to all the main characters; each has a "first death," but then also a second. For Miro, of course, his intended "first death" is Kate, his sacrificial victim. But it is Artkin's death that turns out instead to be his first, and Kate's his second. Kate has had a pseudo-death from choking long before her real death at Miro's hand. Ben has been "buried" twice, once at Fort Delta after his suicide and once in his father's mind. Both Artkin and the general have died morally and emotionally in their commitment to fanaticism and both die later because of their sons, although the general's "death" is not literal. Cormier has said in an interview: "There are so many deaths, you know? Death of innocence, the real deaths, but once there is that first death, it is so devastating that the others pale beside it. It's very intriguing to me, along with the sense that we are dying all the time and killing all the time. Not only with guns."[2]

Cormier traces the genesis of *After the First Death* to several threads of inspiration. One idea that was much in his mind at that time was the parent-child relationship. Renee was an adoring twelve-year-old, and he was very conscious of trying to live up to her exalted concept of her father. But he pondered on how terrible it would be if a parent should manipulate a child by using that unquestioning admiration. A second and unrelated thread was a character he had had in mind for years, whom he had dubbed the California Girl. "You find her everywhere—in Massachusetts, New York—She's that lovely, terrific blonde, a cheerleader maybe—that always has a date for the prom. You see her walk down the street and she's lovely to look at, she brightens your day just for that moment." He had always wanted to write about such a young woman and to explore the complications and hidden defects that he suspected lay beneath the bright surface. Then a third thread: "I read about an incident of a bomb being thrown in a post office where innocent children were killed indiscriminately. And I thought, what kind of person could possibly do this? It had to go beyond villainy. . . . An act like that could only be done out of a sense of innocence. A terrible, terrible kind of innocence." Terrorists, he noticed, always went to other places. What reason could they have to come to New England? Then one day, driving by Fort Devens, he got his answer. "In the sky loomed these planes. They were like ugly vultures. From the bowels of the planes came these evil eggs that blossomed into parachutes. It was somehow very ominous to me. And I realized that this Army installation fifteen miles away has always been a brooding presence in our lives." And what secrets could be hidden there, secrets valuable to terrorists?

"And then came the characters . . . Artkin and Miro . . . and they began to clash against each other, and I knew that they *had* to snatch that bus, and the first thing they had to do was *kill that bus driver*, that retired man who'd been doing it—But it turned out that it just had to be that driver's day off and here came this lovely girl. And I thought, Finally, I'm going to write a love story. This boy Miro is awakening to sexuality, awakening to life, he's a complete innocent (as monstrous as his innocence is) and here's Kate, who feels that she's been untested—she, too, is just opening like a flower, she's questioning herself—and I thought, here's a chance where they'll get together."[3] But it was not to be just that way. Again the inevitability of plot carried the story to a dark ending.

This same irresistible current swept him in painful directions. It dawned on him at some point that at least one child would have to be killed violently by the terrorists. He recoiled, but realized it would have to be. Putting it off as long as he could, he finally wrote Raymond's death, and then went back and developed the character. In retrospect he realized he had done it in this order to spare himself the pain of killing a child he knew.[4] To the reader also Raymond's death is almost unbearable, partly because Cormier has made the character so entrancing. Sketched in two paragraphs and a few lines of dialogue, Raymond comes vividly alive: chubby, intelligent, poignant in his confused sorrow at being a "late child," whispering to Kate in his deep old-man's voice or sneaking a peek at the bad guys with one bright eye.

The other minor characters are also interesting beyond plot necessity. Little Monique is touching in her dream about her Classie, cute but recognizably a real child. On the other end of the scale, Stroll and Antibbe, the third and fourth terrorists, are menacing cartoons—inhuman but interesting. Stroll, the black who drives as if he were conducting a symphony, is so silent that he can convey a whole lecture of disapproval merely by shifting his position at the window. His name suggests utter coolness during strife. Antibbe is a grim Hardy to his somber Laurel—"His grimace could be like thunder rumbling, his frown an earthquake. He lumbered through life like a freight car on the loose."

Antibbe's name, like those of Miro and Artkin, is meant to evoke a generalized—but not a specific—Middle Eastern country.[5] (But of course these are chosen, not given names.) Of the homeland, we know only that it is now controlled by a foreign power, the women are dark and modestly veiled, and, as Miro quotes poetically, "the orange trees are fruitful and the flight of the turtle dove and the lark is balm to the eyes and spirit. The river there is gentle and the sun is a blessing on the earth and turns the flesh golden. The sky is the blue of shells washed by fresh rains." Cormier has no intention of taking sides in any actual political controversy; he has more important and more eternal matters to consider.

Kate herself, Cormier's California Girl, goes far beyond the stereotype of the pretty blonde teenager. In a brilliant stroke, Cormier has hit on the perfect device to humanize her—the shameful secret of her weak bladder. Kate's wet panties make us forgive her for being otherwise physically perfect, make us willing to listen sympathetically to her struggle to be brave. Because Kate—uncertain as she is of the fact even to the last—*is* brave. But it is a self-defeating bravery because she doesn't believe in it. She short-circuits all her chances to escape. Artkin looks at her in anger, and she sees "flat, dead eyes, as if they had no life at all except what they reflected. . . ." Those implacable eyes convince her that her gestures of bravery must be futile, and so futile they are. Artkin is certainly implacable, but, as the reader knows, he is not all-powerful, and Kate has many opportunities. She might have thrown the ignition key out the window before they reached the bridge, an idea that does occur to her momentarily but one that she rejects. She might have darted out the emergency door before Antibbe locked it or tried to escape when Miro allowed her to empty the pail outside. Or she might have made better use of Raymond's alertness by planning a way for him to help her overpower Miro. Her one real escape attempt need not have ended when the engine stalled; there was still time to start the bus again, but Kate gives up immediately and even presses the lever herself that lets the terrorists back in the bus. Instead of active resistance she falls back on the one power play her short life has taught her is always effective—she puts all her energy into trying to use her sexuality to manipulate a man. At the end, when she knows better, she still keeps on with her misguided efforts to wheedle her way out of a bad situation, and by going too far, brings on her own death. She is even denied the heroism that might have been hers if Artkin had accepted her flamboyant demand to take Raymond's place—but she knows he won't. Kate is brave, but not very smart about it.

Ben, by contrast, is a victim from the beginning. Nettie, the girl who rejects him, sees this quality as clearly as if he had a "Kick Me" sign hung around his neck, and acts accordingly. His innocence, the general tells him, made him perfect for the role he had to play. He admires his father blindly and does his bidding without question, and when confronted by the implacable, he gives up immediately, willingly. The only resistance he can offer at last is the angry symbolic gesture of self-destruction. (Cormier was to explore this idea of suicide as ultimate resistance later in *The Bumblebee Flies Anyway*.) Ben's name conveys sadness to Cormier. He has had "a special feeling for its haunting, evocative powers" ever since he read Thomas Wolfe's lamentation for his brother Ben.[6]

Four interlocking themes are explored in *After the First Death*: betrayal of trust, identity masked or disguised, innocence as evil, and patriotism as fanaticism.

Betrayal of trust appears, as Millicent Lenz has pointed out, in three different central incidents. Each has an ironic dimension. The first is Ben's betrayal under torture of his father's trust by giving away the supposed time of the attack. The irony, of course, is that what the father has actually trusted in is Ben's weakness, and by collapsing under "the fingers" he has fulfilled his father's mission, not betrayed it. The general has set *himself* up for a parallel situation by volunteering to be a public scapegoat if the attack fails. He is willing, as he later explains to Ben, to subject himself to unearned public disgrace just as he has subjected Ben to it. But he fails to notice the crucial difference: he knows he is not a traitor. Ben doesn't. Miro sees "the look of the betrayer" in Ben's eyes. "It was beyond terror or horror or pain. A look of such anguish, such regret. As if he suddenly saw his true doom, a doom that went beyond the fingers, beyond even death. A look that left the boy hollow, empty. A look that said: What have I done?"

Miro remembers that look when, like Ben, he thinks he has betrayed his father. By grabbing for an escaping Kate rather than shouting a warning to Artkin of the approaching soldiers Miro feels he has caused Artkin's death. This guilt is intensified unbearably when Kate convinces him that Artkin was his father. The irony is that in all probability he was not. Nevertheless, Kate dies for this dubious insight, and Miro kills in himself all human emotion. "He would keep himself empty, like before." As Lenz concludes, "Miro's 'suicide' is a suicide of his emotional nature; his 'survival' is terrible, in that he lives on as an automaton programmed to kill for the sake of his cause."

The general, Lenz says, betrays Ben "when he negates his identity as his son and makes him into a pawn for the sake of patriotism."[7] As he mourns later, "I had to forget you were my son." The incident recalls the biblical story of Abraham and Isaac.[8] God tested the patriarch's devotion to Him by ordering Abraham to take his son Isaac into the wilderness and there make of him a burnt offering. Abraham's obedience is perfect. He does exactly as he has been ordered, and only God's intervention at the last minute keeps Isaac from being an unknowing sacrifice like Ben to a higher cause. The irony is that the story in the Bible is meant to show approval of Abraham's unquestioning willingness to make of his son a tool to demonstrate his beliefs. The stone that Ben carries to the terrorists has biblical symbolism, too. In Matthew 7:9 we read: "What man of you, if his son asks him for a loaf, will give him a stone?" Again, ironically, the quotation illustrates the loving protection of the Fatherhood of God.

Hidden and disclosed identity is a recurring theme with Cormier. He returns again and again to play with the idea—in *I Am the Cheese*, in *Bumblebee*, in the unpublished "Rumple Country," and in *After the First Death*. Here the symbol is the mask—the knitted ski hoods that Artkin and Miro don to hide their faces, but that paradoxically reveal their evil by showing only the cruel eyes and mouths. Kate reads her own fate in the masks because she knows that they will never let her live now that she has seen their real faces: "She knew she was doomed. She had known it the moment she saw them put on the masks." Miro both loves and hates the mask. "Sometimes . . . he felt like a prisoner in the mask, as if he were locked inside, looking out at the world but not part of it." Yet he loves the sense of power and authority it gives him. "Men's faces paled when they confronted him in the mask, men many years older and much bigger and stronger." But he broods about the mask because "he had the feeling that he must be doing something dishonorable if the operations and confrontations had to be carried out with faces hidden. If what we are doing is heroic . . . why must we hide who we are?" Artkin's answer is that "they had to disguise themselves to remain free under the wrong laws." In disguise Miro then finds meaning, but also another question: "Without the mask, he was Miro Shantas, the boy without even a real name to identify him to the world. With the mask, he was Miro Shantas, freedom fighter. He often wondered which person he really was."

Kate too has disguises. Her public self is the blonde, ever-smiling cheerleader, but behind that shiny identity that she presents so carefully to the world she senses other unexplored selves. "All the Kate Forresters. Were other people like that, she wondered, not simply one person but a lot of them mixed together? Did the real person finally emerge? But suppose that real person turned out to be someone terrible? Or someone who never found love?" The risk is too much.

The general also hides his identity, by merging with his dead son. In addition, like Artkin and Miro, he has a false name that represents his patriotic self: General Rufus Briggs. The mystic power of names is suggested in several places. The name of the dead child is unknown at first; Kate's involvement with the children is intensified as she unwillingly sorts out their names; she is reluctant to know the name of the big man breaking the bus window, and when Artkin chooses to kill the little boy who didn't eat the candy, but is unable to remember his name, Kate tries to protect Raymond by refusing to tell it. Most of all, there is the strange moment when Artkin, to show Miro that he must completely submerge his old identity and the name that went with it, delicately leads the dim-witted waitress to the place where she doubts her own name and for a second her own selfhood.

This toying with the idea of hidden identity and names leads up to the central theme of *After the First Death*. "The monstrous," says Cormier, "is so often disguised as innocence."[9] Although all the characters are "innocent" in one sense or another, it is Miro who most clearly illustrates the idea of innocence as evil. At first Kate sees him as simple, like an animal—"a dog straining at a leash." Only gradually does she uncover the extent of his corruption. MacLeod says:

> The tentative human relationship created between them when Kate encourages Miro to talk about his past dissolves abruptly when Kate recognizes the depth and the terrible simplicity of Miro's dedication to his political purpose. For the sake of a country he has never seen, and never really expects to see, Miro has made himself into an instrument of guerrilla warfare. Save for his mentor, Artkin, he has no connection with the actual world of human life, nor does he expect any. He envisions no future for himself, takes no interest in his own qualities except as they make him an efficient weapon in a struggle whose political terms he cannot possibly know. He has no feeling for the innocent victims, past or potential, of the undeclared "war" he wages; indeed, he cannot even understand what it is Kate expects him to feel for them.[10]

Kate is deeply shocked by this revelation. "And the greatest horror of all was that he did not know he was a monster. He had looked at her with innocent eyes as he told her of killing people. She had always thought of innocence as something good, something to cherish. People mourned the death of innocence. . . . But innocence, she saw now, could also be evil."

To himself Miro seems not guilty but brave and right. As Cormier explained in a discussion of terrorism, "what does he see when he looks in the mirror that night? Not evil. We rationalize our sins, even as we confess them. Who looks into a mirror and says: I'm the bad guy? But the bomber is the bad guy, evil made flesh, and he can live with himself and continue his fatal work only if he is convinced that what he is doing is good. He must be innocent in his own soul. Thus, just as patriotism can reach a point where it becomes evil, so can evil also blossom into innocence."[11]

Artkin and the general are innocent in the sense of "not guilty"—in their own eyes. Both feel that their side is supremely right and the others are always wrong, and anything done in the name of that right is justifiable. In this surrender of moral judgment they have also surrendered their humanity. Once the total commitment to the cause is made, all other choices vanish. The general describes his patriotism as "pure and sweet and unquestioning. We were the good guys. . . . This generation looks at itself in a mirror as it performs its duties. And wonders: Who are the good guys? Is it possible we are the bad guys? They should never ask that question, Ben, or even contemplate it."

This fanaticism blinds them to normal human emotions of love and joy and pity. Artkin, in a hideous parody of compassion, "had often said they were not interested in needless cruelty. They had a job to do and the job concerned death. Do not prolong it more than necessary. Deliver it as efficiently as possible with the least mess. We are not animals, after all, he said, but merely a means to an end. Everything is done for a purpose." But Kate sees the truth clearly when she cries out just before her death, "What the hell has purpose got to do with living or dying?"

The general is neither more nor less evil than Artkin; each is capable of anything in the name of patriotism. There are no limits—killing a child, sacrificing a son—they are a pair. The general sees this plainly: "We knew each other across the chasm; we had recognized each other across the ravine, although we had never met." Artkin, too, understands that the general is a fellow-fanatic, and even gives grudging admiration to the extent of his madness: "Either you are a great patriot or a great fool." And the general answers, "Perhaps both." In the end remorse overtakes the father for the sacrifice of the son, and in this there is hope.

In a way Artkin is an exaggerated reflection of the general, just as Emile is a caricature of Archie in *The Chocolate War*. Artkin's fanaticism is a warning, the logical end result of such a total commitment. The general is for us the more dangerously seductive figure because to some degree we agree with his cause and are in danger of justifying his actions. He moves, after all, through the landscape of American patriotism—Lexington, Concord—and it is our own country he thinks he is defending. Artkin ponders, "Who knows about Americans? Perhaps they cherish their children more than their agencies." But it soon becomes clear that the safety of the children—or of any of us—is not really the central concern. The institution preserves itself—mindlessly, mercilessly—at all costs.

"Cormier," said *Publishers Weekly*, "bases his flawless tragedy on a plot as ancient as the slingshot, as modern as the H-bomb." *After the First Death* is "a work of art which like Picasso's 'Guernica' and Goya's 'Disasters of War' stands as a passionate indictment of inhumanity."[12]

Los Angeles Times, Sunday, 27 April 1980:

> . . . By all reports the American rescue force sent to Iran was part of a special counterterrorist unit that was formed and directed at Ft. Bragg. . . .
>
> Although neither the Pentagon nor Ft. Bragg authorities will confirm that the raiders trained at this base, enlisted men here say that such a group, known as the Delta Team, was directed by the John F. Kennedy Institute and Center for Military Assistance here. . . .
>
> Officials at the Kennedy Center and at Ft. Bragg headquarters refuse to discuss the Delta Team or its operations. "It's just something that's not been discussed around here," Maj. Thomas V. Woods, the chief information officer for Ft. Bragg, said. "It's all new to me today—Delta, the nickname Blue Light. I'm not authorized to say anything." . . .
>
> None of the soldiers knew many details of Delta's operations. "Delta? That's top secret," one enlisted man said. "They don't spill the beans around here."[13]

9. The Early Novels and Short Stories

The four dark young adult novels—*The Chocolate War, I Am the Cheese, After the First Death*, and *Beyond the Chocolate War*—form a tetralogy of political statement and are undoubtedly Cormier's mature masterpieces. The brilliant and complex structure, the intricate wordplay and subtlety of thought, and above all the power and conviction of theme are unequaled by anything of his that came before or has yet come after. Of all Cormier's early short stories and adult novels, only *Now and at the Hour* comes close to conveying this dark vision with such mastery. It is interesting and sometimes enlightening, however, to look at these works for sources of characters and incidents and insights into his themes.

Even Cormier's first published story, "The Little Things That Count," gives an indication of directions to come. Written when he was only nineteen and published in *Sign*, a Catholic family magazine, it is undeniably sentimental, even corny. It shows a young writer deeply steeped in conventional Catholicism. But it has the characteristic Cormier poignance, the twist of the heart at happiness remembered.

Young Joe is musing over some scenes from his childhood. "Funny, the things a fellow thinks of. Why, he had not looked back upon them for years. It seemed he had been too busy with the important things in life." He recalls his terror at his first day of school and how he cried when he was left by his mother in the charge of a nun. "Joe thought she looked wicked in the black robes. He was afraid of her for a long time." But then there was another day when the sunlight through the church's stained glass, the thunder of the organ, and the priest at the altar gave him a glimpse into the real meaning of faith. At ten Joe wanted to be a cowboy playing his guitar as he rode across the plains; a gift of a real guitar punctured the dream. Then there was Anne Marie, the most beautiful girl in the fifth grade. The day he kissed her on the school steps was pure happiness—until the sister saw them and said harsh, cruel things that made him feel dirty. Later his beloved mother fell ill and he promised the Holy Virgin Mary he would always wear a blue tie in her honor if only his mother would get well. The Virgin granted his prayer, but then his mother explained to him that God's mercy is given freely, and not in exchange for promises. Joe remembers getting ready for his first high-school prom amid the admiration and encouragement of his family, and the perfect moment of anticipation as he set out for the dance.

Then comes a trick ending of the kind that was much admired in the 1940s, an "O. Henry twist." It changes the reader's attitude to what has gone before and sends him back to the beginning to read the first paragraph with new understanding. "Funny, the things a fellow thinks of. Not the big, important times in life, but little, crazy moments that were half lost in laughter and tears. And it was of these little things that he thought as he lay in the foxhole during the hour before he died." Obvious as this simple attempt at irony is, it clearly anticipates the far more sophisticated surprises of the circular last chapters of *I Am the Cheese*.

The story is autobiographical in several ways. The celebration of a loving family and the search for a deeper understanding of God were intensely important to young Bob at this age. The details of the church recall St. Cecelia's of French Hill—the sunlight through the windows and the hymns sung in French. The picture of the nuns as grim black presences is also drawn from Cormier's childhood perceptions, and was to reappear often in his later work. Most significantly, when young Joe runs to fetch his father from a union meeting because his mother is sick, he happens to hear a speaker on the platform say, "I'm just a peaceful man, but it is time to fight," and the words stay in his memory long afterward. The sentence is meant to foreshadow Joe's identity as a soldier, and as such it is a device that is more subtle than the rest of this simple story. But it also is a startlingly precise statement of the central theme that would occupy Cormier's mature powers.

Until the publication of *The Chocolate War* Cormier continued to write short stories although, as he himself recognized, he is not at his best in the form. The retrospective collection that appeared in book form in 1980 under the unimaginative title *Eight Plus One* is a fairly typical selection of his later stories. They were written between 1965 and 1975, the years when Cormier's own children were in their teens, and the protagonists of four of the nine stories are fathers. The publishers—and the author himself—stressed that this book showed "Robert Cormier from a different angle—warm, touching, and intensely personal."[1] It may be that they felt that it was expedient to defuse the growing controversy about the bleakness of his novels by presenting him in another, more genial, light. In any case, the attempt to resurrect these slight and somewhat dated stories was ill-timed. Cormier had developed a readership of young adults who expected something very different from him, and who were puzzled by these stories that were mostly written from a middle-aged point of view and for a middle-aged audience. Trying to close the gap, he wrote short introductions for each story that told a bit about the writer at work. Some critics tried hard out of loyalty to find a reason that the book would be relevant to teenagers. "It may be a refreshing experience for teenagers to read about adolescence, frankly recollected by a sympathetic middle-aged man," suggested *Hornbook*.[2] *Washington Post Book World* tried "a painless but useful introduction for the young reader to the art of fiction."[3] But other critics were not so kind. "Fans . . . will be disappointed," said the *Kirkus Review*, with these ". . . nine tepidly sentimental stories."[4] Benjamin De Mott, writing in the *New York Times*, was particularly savage: "an ill-written cliché-infested book awash in self-pity, and I can't think of a 'young adult' anywhere upon whom

I'd be willing to inflict it."[5] Cormier's own reputation was a handicap to him in the reception of this book, as *School Library Journal* noted regretfully: "none of the tales are as dramatic as Cormier's brilliant and imaginative novels."[6]

In the long view, the real value of *Eight Plus One* is in the light it sheds on Cormier's later work. Take, for example, the origins of the familiar episode of the girl at the bus stop. The essence of the incident goes something like this: a boy sees a beautiful girl on the street and admires her from afar. Something in her manner finally gives him hope and he gets up the nerve to call her on the phone, only to be devastated by her rejection. This incident recurs often in Cormier's work, serving usually to dramatize the state of the narrator's self-esteem. In *The Chocolate War* Jerry yearns after the girl he sees every day at the bus stop, but when he finally spies out her phone number and calls her, she has no idea who he is. In *After the First Death* Ben/Mark falls in love with Nettie Haversham at first meeting and mistakes her vivacity for encouragement, but on the phone she responds to his request for a date with a laconic "Oh, I don't think so." Adam's call to Amy also leads to frustration and then rejection, not by Amy herself but by the older man who now lives at that number. In *Eight Plus One* the motif appears in a story called "Guess What? I Almost Kissed My Father Goodnight," a story first published in 1971, three years before *The Chocolate War*. A teenage boy is smiled at by a pretty girl, Sally Bettencourt, at a bus stop. When he follows up with a phone call, she is polite but doesn't know him, and even calls him by the wrong name at the end of the conversation. Then in the introduction to "Another of Mike's Girls" we discover a hint of the original emotion that must have given this scene its fascination for Cormier: "I still remember vividly the impact of a *but*—that monster of a word . . .—pronounced on the lips of a girl I was hopelessly in love with in the ninth grade: *I think you're a swell guy, Bob, but—*"

The idea that heroes are not always rewarded, even by themselves, and that a virtuous self-sacrifice doesn't necessarily lead to happiness was presented with devastating effect in *The Chocolate War*. An earlier and much gentler version of that concept is the point of a story called "President Cleveland, Where Are You?" A young boy gives up the possibility of winning a coveted baseball glove so that he can help his older brother buy the girl he loves a corsage for the big dance. That evening, with darkness coming on, he remembers, "I sat there a long time, waiting for the good feeling to come."

Three of the stories are set in the depression years and deal with family life in Frenchtown from the point of view of the second son in a large family. Five are about fathers set in the late 1960s and early 1970s, and two are told by teenage boys. The material is obviously drawn from Cormier's childhood in French Hill and his later years as the suburban father of a family of teenagers, as he himself explains in the introductions. This autobiographical element is especially interesting for Cormier fans, and he adds to it with anecdotes and bits of description, such as the words about his own father in the preface to "Guess What? I Almost Kissed My Father Goodnight."

The glimpses of the writer behind the scenes are intriguing. He explains the importance to him of a second, or symbolic level in a story; he traces his discovery of the power of figurative language; he describes his discomfort with changes in titles. Cormier has always been generous in disclosing the mechanics of his composition; as he said once in an interview, he is anxious that young people not "think that books are created by 'writing machines' out there someplace."[7]

Well-crafted and touching as some of these stories are, the final critical judgment has to be that Cormier's pleasant works, characters, and scenes are not memorable. Only in darkness does he show his real power. An examination of the adult novels proves the point.

Intended as a comedy, *Take Me Where the Good Times Are* is the weakest of the three, although it has some wonderful vignettes. It tells the pathetic tale of an old man who, like some elderly Holden Caulfield, runs away from an old-folks' home and spends a disastrous *Catcher in the Rye* twenty-four hours wandering the city in search of some meaning for his life. Tommy Bartin feels trapped and old at the Monument City Infirmary, where he has lived for the last three years, ever since a gall-bladder operation cost him his lifetime job at a comb factory. The other "guests" at the Place, as Tommy calls it, are a collection of grotesques with names that anticipate the inmates of the Complex in *Bumblebee*: Awful Arthur, Sweet Mary, Stretch, Knobby, Hungry Harry, and Annabel Lee, the retarded teenage daughter of the superintendent. Even though the Place is kindly, Tommy yearns to escape back to town to the self-respect of a job. When Sweet Mary dies and secretly leaves him a little money he has the means, and when a gang of motorcycle boys take Annabel Lee away for a wild ride he has the pretext to leave, to look for her. Once in town, "where the good times are," all his attempts to find old friends and his old job end sadly, and each episode sends him scurrying back to Lu's Place for a few more cool ones to drown his memories. A phone call to the Place tells him that Annabel Lee has been found, upset but unhurt, and his resolve to stay in town is strengthened. He finds an old drinking companion, Jean Baptiste La Chapelle, who has been destroyed by loneliness, and when Tommy follows him home in concern he finds that his room in a shabby boardinghouse is filled with dolls, Baptiste's imaginary companions. There is a hilarious encounter when the now very drunk Tommy drops in on a meeting of the Happy Timers, an old-folks social club, and scandalizes them by reading bawdy poems. At last he tracks down the motorcycle boys in a bar, and the leader, Rudy, cajoles him into downing a drink that has been spiked with knock-out drops. Tommy wakes up the next morning in the canvas-shrouded lap of a statue about to be dedicated before a Memorial Day crowd. With what little dignity he has left he stands up straight at attention as the canvas is pulled off. "There's a time when a man shouldn't do a thing but take his medicine, a time when a man fights back by doing nothing." But the effect is spoiled when he falls off the pedestal. Later, in the hospital the folks from the Place urge him to come back. He gives in, but still full of spunk, he plans to do it better next time he escapes. As he tells himself, "a man can admit that he's seventy years of age but that doesn't mean the sun isn't going to come up tomorrow."

Although a few scenes are worth a smile, the general effect is sad rather than amusing. *Kirkus Review* perhaps overstated it a bit by saying "the aching verities of a past forever lost are almost too painful to bear in this passionate recording of the pathetic odyssey of an old man."[8] Tommy is not very likable—a selfish and foolish old geezer, very slow to give up his delusions—and it seems mean to laugh at him. Only his tender longing for his dead wife and his compassion for the retarded Annabel Lee redeem him, and in the end he has learned nothing. He is only waiting his chance to go out and thumb his nose at old age all over again. Which is foolishly touching—but not funny.

Rudy, the leader of the motorcycle gang, is a derivative character, a two-dimensional echo of Marlon Brando in *The Wild One* and of countless other head bikers in the films of the late 1950s. But certain aspects of the stereotype foreshadow the more original wickedness of Cormier's later villains. When Rudy gets his kicks from telephone calls in which he helpfully informs women that their husbands have just been seen having sex in the back seat of a car, we are reminded of Emile's silly and pointless cruelties. In Rudy's exaggerated politeness and false friendliness toward Tommy there is that sweet and terrible gentleness evil reserves for the victim, a gentleness that we have seen in Brother Leon's tormenting of his students, in Artkin's preparing to deliver death, and in Archie's giving of an assignment—he who "always treated them with tenderness, as if a bond existed between them." And when Rudy stands in the Memorial Day audience as the trembling Tommy is revealed on the statue, he, like Archie, feels like a proud creator before the evil he has done.

This book, and the one that preceded it, *A Little Raw on Monday Mornings*, gave Cormier for a time a critical reputation as the novelist of the "little people." As *America* magazine said, "to chronicle the small pleasures, the larger troubles and the rare triumphs of the somewhat seedy poor in such a way as to make the characters interesting and even strangely attractive is no small achievement."[9] This smug judgment missed the central fact of Cormier's work: its universality. The troubles he writes about are not the exclusive property of "the somewhat seedy poor"—they belong to all of us, with only slight changes of circumstances. In the case of *A Little Raw on Monday Mornings*, however, it is easy to make this mistake, because its surface reflects so faithfully the people and places and attitudes of Cormier's working-class French Hill background. Father W. B. Hill, writing in *Best Seller* magazine, admitted that it showed "a rare sort of artistic integrity" but complained that "it is so plain at times that it is a bit tiring; the reality is obvious, familiar, and occasionally a bit flat."[10]

Gracie is a crashingly ordinary middle-aged woman whose life for the past three years has been sliding downhill, ever since her twelve-year-old daughter was murdered and her husband drank himself to death in sorrow. She moves numbly through the routine of her drab life, putting in long days at the plastics factory and trying tiredly to do the best she can to raise her remaining three children decently. She has tried to make herself "hard" to other people—as her grim television-addicted mother has always urged her—and now finds it difficult to stop alienating her teenage daughter Dorrie with her coldness. One night, in a mood for once for a little relief from the grimness of her life, she goes to a neighborhood bar to drink and dance with some others from the factory. A few rare moments of happiness with the music and the beer, a surrender to self-pity, and a memory of tenderness—and in the morning Gracie is pregnant by Bert, a weak, rather repulsive forty-year-old "floor boy" from the factory. Although she is shamed and repelled by the idea of marriage with Bert, he is not too averse to it, and so they begin to form a tentative relationship, which ends abruptly when his family persuades him to run away. Violating her Catholic principles, Gracie goes to Boston for an abortion, but finds she cannot go through with it. In her agonized struggles with her problem she begins to find that there are occasional moments when she can reach out to her daughter and to her mother. At last she does what she must, goes after a not unwilling Bert and asks him to come back so that they can make the best of it.

This dog-eared story has a sweetness in its honesty—although Cormier allows no compromise for the characters or the reader. The portrayal of Gracie is affecting, and the perceptiveness with which she is drawn is an answer to those who accuse Cormier of an inability to write convincing female characters. The details are exactly right: the aches of Gracie's body from the workbench or the too-tight girdle, the weariness of soul from a sinkful of dirty dishes in the early morning or a child's shirt to be ironed at midnight, the small vanities with which she clings to her vanishing femininity. Gracie wears high heels even on a visit to the cemetery because she thinks her legs look too heavy in flat shoes, and one of the reasons she goes to the bar that night is that "her hair had come out beautiful at the beauty shop."

All the characters of *A Little Raw on Monday Mornings* are intensely Catholic. Their belief in the ritual requirements of the Church and the catechism they were taught as children is fervent, if a bit haphazard in execution. "Mr. Cormier's characters," observed *Library Journal*, "all live out their lives in an anguish engendered by their conviction of spiritual realities."[11] Gracie's religion gives her a great deal of guilt and very little comfort. In the end she finds strength only within herself, as she picks up her cards without whining to play the hand life has dealt her.

Although the whole setting is autobiographical, there is one incident that is especially striking in its connection to Cormier's own life. Bert in his youth has had an impressive singing voice, so much so that he is invited to perform on an amateur hour on television. He stands before the cameras and five million viewers and opens his mouth and his mind goes blank. When he does manage to croak out a few notes, the whole song is off key. He never performs again, until years later in Gracie's living room, when as a gift of trust he offers to sing for her. The piece he chooses is "Little Old Lady"—the song that young Bob Cormier intended to sing on the operating table before the oxygen mask cut him off.

Old age, unwanted pregnancy—many human beings must face them and keep their dignity as best they can. But the most universal Implacable, the one we all must face, is death. The fictional literature of death in the English language is a very small body of work. True, a lot of dying goes on in fiction. But actually to contemplate just what it might feel like to die, to look oncoming death straight in the eye, is too terrible to imagine for all but the bravest writers. There are novels about suicide and novels about violent death in war, but those are special cases, and more romantic than the way most of us expect to go. Even James Agee's great *A Death in the Family* is about the survivors, not the deceased. So Cormier's first book, *Now and at the Hour*, stands almost alone as a novel about an ordinary man getting ready to die a natural death.

At first Alph LeBlanc thought it was going to be all right. He had had to retire from the comb factory after the operation for lung cancer, but that meant time for rides in the car he had finally bought last year, time to spend with his good, comfortable wife, Ellie, and their five grown kids. But then the pain started and the doctor said the tumor had spread to his arm. One afternoon Alph wakes from a nap with a terrible realization. "The knowledge overwhelmed him, partly lifting him from the bed as a wave lifts a man. His hands roved wildly over the blankets, seeking something to grip, to hold on to for support. He tried to deny the thought, to turn from it. But it was more than a thought—it was a deep, certain knowledge that had welled up inside, like an evil flower blossoming. It was a knowledge that had been there all the time, waiting to push toward the surface. He wasn't going to get better."

His family knows. He can hear it in their bright, cheerful false voices. He hardens his courage to hide his knowledge from them, to give them the gift of pretense. He knows that if he crumbles by seeking comfort from them something will be gone from him. So Alph endures alone, through the bad days and the good days, the days when he has hope that it is not true, and the days when he knows with terror that it is. Gradually he loses strength and life and has to accept the diminishing indignities of illness. "In his clear moments, he felt a sense of everything getting narrow. He thought of how his world had narrowed, from the outside of the house to the inside and then to this room and then his bed and now his body."

Alph looks back on his life with Ellie, the time when his children were little, and the humble landmarks of those years: the great day he won fifty dollars at beano; the terrible death of his three-year-old daughter; in later years the buying of the house and the car. He is afraid that he has failed those he loved, because he has been able to do so little for them. But then one day his daughter Doris tells him how much it meant to her as a frightened child to wake up at night and know he might be sitting up watching over her, and he realizes that just being there has been enough.

He hangs on tightly to his determination to fight his battle alone, and in his mind he cries out for solace from God, going over and over the old prayers in French he had learned as a child. When the priest is sent for and he makes his last confession he finds only temporary peace, but at the last he finds a scrap of comfort in the thought that Jesus, too, suffered death as a man. One last time he almost gives in to the need for Ellie's pity when she holds him in her arms, but the moment passes and he is safe when he finds he can no longer speak. Death comes, and "he lifted his vacant, ruined face to the night."

Now and at the Hour is a devastating accomplishment, absolutely unflinching in its insistence on the plain details of suffering. In this book Cormier allows himself not one shred of sentimentality or morbidity. Alph is a simple man, and his thoughts contain no great profundities. With him we hurt and dread and grasp at hope, and finally die. That is all.

There is great art here, but it doesn't call attention to itself. The story seems to be told completely without literary artifice. What metaphors and allusions there are grow naturally out of the narrative. The name LeBlanc—"the white" in French—reflects Alph's innocence. The period of his suffering lasts through Lent and ends, like that of his Lord, with Easter. In this and in other details the hope of the resurrection is suggested: the forsythia and then the lilac blooming outside his bedroom window and symbolizing the end of winter, the fresh new life of his grandchildren and the longed-for pregnancy of one of his daughters. The bedside clock is a symbol first of Alph's retirement and liberation from its alarm, and then comes to be associated with pain and the intervals of time between pills, and at last represents the minutes of his life draining away.

The title, of course, is from the last line of the Hail Mary: "Pray for us . . . now and at the hour of our death." Cormier had wanted to call it "Every Day They Die among Us," a line from the W. H. Auden poem "In Memory of Sigmund Freud":

> Of whom shall we speak? For every day they die
> Among us, those who were doing us some good,
> And knew it was never enough but
> Hoped to improve a little by living.

But the publisher felt the phrase would discourage buyers because it contained the word "die." When Cormier protested that the book *was* about death, the publisher replied, "Nevertheless."[12]

The novel inspired reviewers to eloquence. Phoebe-Lou Adams wrote in the *Atlantic*: "It is quite a task to make an interesting hero of a man who has done no great deeds, committed no crimes, suffered no psychological upheavals, never been painfully poor or even mildly rich, and who has in the course of the book nothing to do but think, an activity which he carries on at a quite uncomplicated level and without a trace of imagination. . . . The author . . . ends by creating a touching picture of a man who is not nearly as ordinary as he himself thinks."[13]

Catholic World called it "writing and perceiving of a rare fineness and distinction," and added, "In spite of its subject, it is anything but repellent, for Alph's humanity and his courage—and not his illness—are its center."[14] The reviewer in the *New York Herald Tribune* concluded, "Rising above morbidity and what might have been mere pathos, this sincere and unassuming little book reveals effectively the essential dignity and worth in the living and dying of a simple man."[15]

Robert Cormier is not a simple man. Twenty-three years later, he again used the approach of death as the subject for a novel. This time, with five other novels of increasing complexity and scope marking his progress as a writer, the conclusion was very different—but also very much the same.

10. *The Bumblebee Flies Anyway*

Again it is spring, and there is dying going on. A whole hospital full of dying. Barney Snow—Bernard Jason Snow—has a name that, like LeBlanc, symbolizes his "whiteness," his innocence. But much more. Snow is cold, like death, like a lack of love. "Your heart is as cold as your name," says his friend Billy the Kidney —but he knows it isn't true. Barney's actions are compassionate toward the other inmates of the Complex, an experimental hospital for the terminally ill. He just doesn't want to talk about anybody's past, because—even though he can't admit it to himself—he has no memories of his own to share. His mind is full of "blankness, like snow, suffocating, obliterating snow." The Handyman, as he calls the director of the pediatric unit, has warned Barney to stay in his own emotional "compartment" and to avoid entanglements with the other "guests," because, after all, he is the control, the only one here who is not dying. Barney Snow is being snowed.

The story begins the day that Ronson gets the Ice Age—an experiment with cold in which he is strapped down and hooked up to a lot of "doodads" and shot full of chill-producing "merchandise." "Doodads" and "merchandise" are Barney's terms for things in the Complex that are too scary to name. The patients here at the Complex are all volunteers who have offered their terminal illnesses for scientific experimentation, to give others the hope *they* cannot have. Even the inmates of Section 12, the pediatric unit, are volunteers: pathetic Billy the Kidney, spastic Allie Roon, the doomed Ronson, and rich, handsome, and obnoxious Mazzo. Barney has been here four or five weeks, time enough for several unpleasant encounters with the merchandise. Although he is not dying, he is to be the subject for some experiments on memory and the brain, the Handyman explains. When they are physically able, the patients are allowed to leave the hospital for short walks. One day Barney, Allie Roon, and Billy the Kidney stroll past a nearby automobile junkyard, and the sight of a red MG among the rusting ruins triggers Barney's recurring nightmare of a wild rainswept ride in a car that is out of control and about to crash. "Tempo, rhythm," he tells himself, a phrase that he uses to invoke calm and control.

Wealthy Mazzo gets a telephone installed in his room, much to Billy's envy, but refuses to answer its ringing when his anxious mother tries to reach him. Seeing Billy's yearning to use the phone, Barney strikes a bargain later with Mazzo. He will stand by in the room when Mazzo's twin sister, Cassie, comes to visit so that she will not be able effectively to persuade Mazzo to see their mother. In return Billy can telephone (although he knows no one to call) for an hour a day. Barney takes one look at beautiful Cassie and is instantly in love with her. She, seeing his adoration, manipulates him into becoming a "tender spy" and giving her daily reports on Mazzo's condition. Barney's love for Cassie awakens him to life again, and also to the fear that memories of her will be swept away in the experiments he is undergoing. A terrifying episode with the merchandise temporarily wipes out all his knowledge of self-identity, but after a few days he is returned to himself, only to learn that the telephone has been a failure for Billy and that Ronson has died. In trying to talk with Mazzo, Barney has learned that the only thing that still interests him is fast cars. Going back to the junkyard, he finds that the red MG is a balsa-wood fake put together by a woodworking class, and he conceives a plan: he will unscrew the parts of the car and sneak it back into the Complex, where he will put it together in the cellar and then take Mazzo for one last wild ride. He shares the plan with Billy and Allie and they are ecstatic at being included in the project.

Meanwhile, several episodes from Cassie's point of view disclose to us (but not to Barney) that her intense interest in her brother's condition is essentially selfish. She has a secret mystic link with him that compels her to suffer in her own body any trauma that happens to him. Now she wonders with dread what will happen to her when he dies.

Barney and the others proceed with the project, but hit a snag when painters arrive to work in the basement. Barney shifts his plan to the attic, where he discovers a skylight opening onto the slanting roof. The plan is transformed: he will give Mazzo a final flight to glory in the car. But as he returns from the attic he idly explores another floor of the complex and finds a corridor, a room, a television monitor that he remembers vividly. He turns the switch and finds that this room is where his nightmare of the rainy car has been created. The Handyman appears and is forced by Barney's panic to reveal that the nightmare—and the phrase "rhythm, tempo" and his fragmentary memories of his mother—have been experimental screens to shield him from his knowledge of a terrible truth: he too is dying of a terminal illness.

Shocked out of remission by the revelation, Barney knows he has not much longer to live. That afternoon, without really meaning to, he tells Cassie about the car, not revealing who the passenger is to be, and she dubs it "the Bumblebee" because, contrary to scientific prediction, it will fly anyway.

Seriously ill now, Barney works frantically against time to finish the car. After a farewell visit with Cassie, that night he and Mazzo, followed by Billy, make the agonized journey to the attic, where they struggle to get the Bumblebee up the stairs to the skylight. The effort is too much for Mazzo, and he dies in Barney's arms before they can push off. Barney realizes he doesn't need to ride, either—it will be enough to see the flight of the Bumblebee. They shove it free—and for a glorious moment it flies.

In two final scenes, Cassie suffers through her twin's death and survives by her own will to live, and Barney, dying in the hospital, continues to exult in his vision of the Bumblebee glowing against the night sky.

That one moment of exaltation and hope as the Bumblebee sails out into space was the goal toward which Cormier worked for several years. The novel was troublesome. "The thing is," he says, "I had the concept. I wanted to have that soaring ending. And I was building up to it, and I would get discouraged. . . . I had times when my words all seemed cumbersome, dull, when it wouldn't get up and dance, when it didn't sing to me, and I knew it was very downbeat, and I didn't know if I could pull it off. At the end. The soaring moment." There is no doubt he has pulled it off. That one chapter is magnificent, unforgettable. But the rest of the novel shows the effects of the not entirely victorious struggle that went into its making.

As with most of Cormier's books, the genesis could be traced to several sources. "It started really one night when I was watching television," he remembers, "and somebody made a brief mention of an experimental hospital in the Midwest, where people with no hope came, hoping they could help others." Intrigued, he began to research it. In the process he came across other medical reports of memory experiments, research on the workings of the brain. Always interested in identity, he turned this new knowledge in that direction. Suppose you were dying, he thought, "and if you couldn't wipe away the disease, suppose you could wipe away the memory of it!" But how much of identity would be the cost of that forgetfulness?

Then there was the poster in his study that explained that "according to the laws of aerodynamics, the bumblebee, because of its heavy body and short wing span, isn't supposed to be able to fly. But the bumblebee, not knowing about this theory or law, flies anyway."[1] The idea of doing the impossible like this had haunted him for years. Writing about the impossible turned out to be nearly as difficult. "The problem was, I knew the car had to be on the roof—now how do I get it there? First I went around researching. I went to junkyards, looked at Volkswagens. . . . Too heavy, too cumbersome. How could a kid get it up there? Okay, so I made it a sports model like an MG. Still too heavy. Then finally I came up with the idea of the mock-up."

And another technical challenge: "I've always wanted to write a straight novel along the lines of a suspense story that would be without crime or violence, but would use the same techniques of false clues and misdirection that you have in a mystery story. That was my intention, to divert the reader from my actual purpose. Have them thinking they're reading one kind of story, and have it turn out that they're reading another kind of story. That's the second level I'm always aiming for." And there was the self-consciousness that came from his sense of responsibility toward his young readers: "When you're writing a book that you know is going to go into a classroom, is going to be dissected, diagrammed, parsed, and argued about, you don't write this casually."

The complex and demanding project almost defeated him. It was five years in the writing. He put it aside in despair for nine or ten months, and then began over again from page 1, finally coming to grips with the problems in the manuscript. Basically, the difficulty revolved—and still does—around the character of Cassie. Reviewers complained that there were flaws in the "depiction of Cassie, who we are told is 'vibrant and compelling,' but who remains an abstraction."[2]

"The major weakness in characterization," they said, "is the portrayal of Cassie, who is convincing as Barney's love idol, but less so as her twin's empathetic alter ego."[3] True, it is understandable that Barney would be completely entranced with Cassie, even if she is not really as "vibrant and compelling" as he thinks. After all, except for a few dim memories of spin-the-bottle at parties, she is the only girl he has ever seen because his past is only five weeks long. But her psychosomatic link with Mazzo *is* puzzling. Aside from the fact of being twins (*nonidentical* twins), they seem to have neither more nor less closeness than the average friendly brother and sister. There is nothing to explain The Thing, nor does Cormier appear to try. It doesn't seem to work as a metaphor, either—it is just pasted onto the story, and because Cassie is basically unlikable, there is only a mild, abstract suspense in wondering if she will be drawn in to Mazzo's death.

Perhaps an explanation was to be found in earlier versions of *Bumblebee*, in which Cassie played a much larger role. According to Cormier, in these first drafts the reader followed Cassie home after her initial encounter with Mazzo and Barney at the Complex. There were chapters and chapters about Cassie's life: her mother and father, her school days, her friends, her later attraction to the religious life. She was seen tagging adoringly after her twin, clapping in the stands for his baseball triumphs, being his "kid sister." Mazzo was sweet to her in those days before he became embittered by his illness, and she admired him because he seemed so sure of what he wanted to do with his life. A healthy Mazzo was very different from the enraged and shallow person that he seems to be in the final version of the book.

Cassie's father, too, was developed, making the brother-sister conflict over the divorce more understandable. He had come to America as an emigrant from Italy. Landing in Boston, he was met by friends who whisked him off to Fenway Park to see a baseball game. Instantly he fell in love with the sport and made it his mission to visit every major league ball park in the country. Whenever his business as owner of a plastics factory allowed, he would make these pilgrimages, and he died fittingly of a heart attack at the base of the statue of Stan Musial outside Busch Stadium in St. Louis.

All of this had to go; it had gotten out of hand. It was becoming a whole other book. Whenever the story left the Complex, the tension Cormier had built so carefully evaporated. But he was entranced with Cassie, especially her fascination with the convent. He had struggled with the character before in the guise of Lily, the young nun who moves through the pages of the unpublished "In the Midst of Winter." Try as he might, he could not make Cassie sympathetic. He even experimented with giving her a saintly aura with the stigmata—the psychomatic re-creation of the wounds of Christ. It didn't work, and he took it out, all except a puzzling fragment. But she needed to be there; the Complex without Cassie was unbearably dreary. She released Barney's aspirations to love and revealed his vulnerabilities; she was the motivation for his closeness to Mazzo and the building of the

Bumblebee. Finally Cormier acceded to the solution suggested by an editor: Cassie was to be seen only through Barney's eyes except where it was absolutely necessary. As published, the book has only four short sections from Cassie's point of view, in which she shows her half-ashamed manipulation of Barney and her terror at The Thing. This way she is lovable at least to Barney, although much about her is unexplained in the truncated version.

An additional problem with *Bumblebee* is the *blankness* of the outer and inner setting: the sterile hospital and Barney's amnesiac mind. By its very nature there can be none of the sweat, noise, collisions, the *events* of, say, *The Chocolate War*. In the Complex everything is silent, bare, colorless, like the empty, drab gray and dull white corridors. The only sounds are the distant humming of machines; all human noises are hushed. "The passage of feet in the halls of the Complex was quiet, muted, footsteps like whispers as patients and staff ghosted by in rubber-soled shoes or slippers." Barney's memory is equally blank, no allusions, anecdotes, connections from the past to anything he sees or feels. Even his senses of taste and smell are gone, and his emotions are deliberately muted and suppressed. This sterility gives the narrative a peculiar flatness of surface. The story moves along on silent rubber-tired wheels like a gurney carrying a patient to surgery. It feels to the reader as if nothing happens at all until the flight of the Bumblebee—which is one reason that moment stands out with such impact.

Outside on the street it is also silent and blank. There is no traffic, no people or houses. The grounds are deserted, neglected, the shrubbery cluttered with wind-blown debris. "Across the street two huge tanks rose against the sky, dwarfing the abandoned building between them. The building had once been a chemical plant. Fire had ravaged the structure, and it stood in disgrace now, charred and blackened, the windows and doors bandaged with wooden boards." Behind the fence in the automobile graveyard there is only the dry death of technology—"this terrible place where the only inhabitant was a gray rat lurking in the ruins." In Barney's drug-distorted mind it becomes a surrealistic vision of Armageddon: "He felt as if he were making his way through a battlefield long after the bombs had exploded and the soldiers had fled, taking the dead and wounded with them." A car door banging in the wind is like the sound of doom. It is the end of the world, the dry dead land without hope of T. S. Eliot's poems "The Hollow Men" and *The Waste Land*. It is the landscape of post-nuclear holocaust.

There are other evocations of nuclear terror in the Complex, reminding us that we, like the other patients, may be facing death in a terminally ill society. The Handyman tells Barney, "There are no guarantees about the future even for the man walking down the street this morning in the best of health, the prime of life." Ronson, going into the Ice Age in Isolation, wears "thermonuclear underwear." Barney, awakening in an otherworldly waiting room after his memory has been completely erased, describes the moment as if it were the neutron bomb: "There had been an explosion of light but no aftermath of smoke and rubble, the way there would be in a real explosion." The automobile graveyard and the Complex are "both filled with busted and broken things." But unfortunately, as Barney reflects, "the junkyard had spare parts and the Complex didn't." Technology can be replaced, but that which is soft and human, once destroyed, is gone forever.

Presiding over this sterile, self-contained place is the enigmatic figure of the Handyman. Who is this Dr. Edward Lakendorp, who has the power of life and death, pain and oblivion over his subjects? Is he evil? The Devil, perhaps, in some existential hell? But hell has no exit, as Sartre made clear, and death is the door here. It is tempting to compare him with Brint from *I Am the Cheese*. Both have mysterious power over the mind with drugs and secrets; both are in hospitals; both speak in euphemisms about painful things. Both are diabolical father confessors to unwilling supplicants. To Barney, the Handyman sometimes looks like a mechanical doll, with hard, cold eyes even when he smiles. But unlike Brint, whose compassion turned out to be a false facade, the Handyman is not a monster. After a talk in which he warns Barney not to allow himself to get too close to Cassie, Barney sees a look on his face as if he were sad and lonely. He can be troubled, make mistakes, suffer from a headache. Barney has been delivered to him; the memory experiments did not begin at the Complex. In some ways he is as much a victim as Barney. So, although he is sometimes made insensitive to suffering by his scientific zeal, he is implacable authority but not evil authority. He is not the enemy.

The Handyman never discusses anything except what goes on in the Complex, Barney notices, "as if no other world existed." That is literally true for the orphan children of Section 12, especially for Barney. Five of Cormier's seven other novels take place in institutions, and in them a steady progression toward equating the Institution with the state of existence itself can be seen: the comical and benevolent old-folks home, the parochial school, the diabolical mental hospital with no escape, the Mafia/government, the international military conspiracy. In *Bumblebee* Cormier has achieved his goal. The Institution is all. Only Mazzo has a link with the world outside, and he won't answer the phone. This connection, which he might use to reach out for comfort and love, is to him only a way to punish. When Billy tries to find human contact over the phone, he finds that it is too late. From inside the Complex they are all wrong numbers.

There are hopeful symbols, too, in this book, which has been called Cormier's most affirmative. On their first excursion to the junkyard, Barney sees a lilac bush growing against the fence, "the purple clusters so heavy they made the branches droop," but it reminds him only that he can no longer smell their fragrance. Bascam, the stiff nurse who keeps the door, has told him to go for a walk and "smell the lilacs," and then blushed at her faux pas. The blooming bush is the only thing soft and alive in the hard stone and metal of the Complex and the junkyard, growing stubbornly in almost no soil.

Lilacs have for American, and particularly New England, poets always been a potent symbol, blossoming as they do at the end of winter. Amy Lowell spoke of them in "Lilacs":

> Your great puffs of flowers
> Are everywhere in this my New England.

Walt Whitman used them as a central symbol of death and returning life in his great elegy for Abraham Lincoln, "When Lilacs Last in the Dooryard Bloom'd." T. S. Eliot turned the symbol inside out with bitter irony in the opening stanzas of *The Waste Land*:

> April is the cruellest month, breeding
> Lilacs out of the dead land. . . .
> What are the roots that clutch, what branches grow
> Out of this stony rubbish?

(Sharp-eyed researchers can verify that Cormier has been here by noting his sly adaptation of the reference to "forgetful snow" that occurs later in the poem. Images from Eliot often pop up in Cormier's work. As we have noted, *The Chocolate War* draws on "The Love Song of J. Alfred Prufrock." An ironic reflection of the malicious children who ambush Jerry can be found in "Burnt Norton":

> The leaves were full of children,
> Hidden excitedly, containing laughter . . .

Poor Ronson hooked up to the Ice Age is suggested in "Prufrock":

> . . . the evening is spread out against the sky
> Like a patient etherized upon a table . . .

And so on.)

Cormier has used the symbol of the lilacs in *Bumblebee*, as he did in *Now and at the Hour*, to affirm the renewal of life and the hope of victory over death. Barney, after his love for Cassie has restored his sense of smell and taste and his appetite for life, returns to the junkyard. This time he sees the lilac bush with new eyes and smells the fragrance. But by now the flowers have begun to fade. Nearby a tree is beginning to sprout tiny pink flowers from its dead-looking branches. "Sad somehow, one life ending while another began. But he drew a kind of comfort from this knowledge, seeing for the first time the continuity of life, nature at work in the world, providing a never-ending process of life in all its forms. Maybe there was some kind of continuity in people, too. Nature at work in people. Or was it God?" He tries to pray, but that knowledge has been almost obliterated with the rest of his memory. He thinks of the bush slumbering through the winter. "Were people like that, too? Death only a sleep from which they eventually awakened? Not the body, of course, but the soul, soaring into eternity, joining others there?" A moment later he climbs the fence and sees the MG once more. A glimmer grows in his mind: ". . . he let the vision burst full flower. He saw for the first time the flight of the Bumblebee. . . ."

Through the symbolism of the lilacs, Barney gropes for the faith in an afterlife that has been erased from his mind. Only fragments of the structure of belief remain—a snatch of a prayer, a brief memory of religious instruction from a nun. "A face flashed before him, pale face enclosed in some kind of starched white collar that concealed ears and hair, and lips moving, saying something about heaven, hell." The dogma is gone, and he is left with only the most banal religious ideas. To comfort Billy's sorrow at Ronson's death Barney conjures up a childish vision of heaven: "Maybe Ronson right this minute is boxing away someplace, winning the championship." But he tells himself it is ridiculous, stupid. After he learns that he is dying, the Handyman in pity offers to bring a priest. Barney suddenly remembers that he has been Catholic, but the candles, the wafer, the alter no longer have meaning for him. He finds that he has clothed his faith with the words "tempo, rhythm," the screen that the Handyman has instilled in his mind to comfort his fear of death. But the outer shape doesn't matter —it is still prayer, it is still faith.

In an amazingly obtuse review in the *Washington Post Book World*, Thomas M. Disch jumped to the conclusion that Cormier had dealt with the fear of death "entirely outside a religious context. His dying youths die without benefit of clergy and with no consolation of faith in an afterlife." In Barney's story of Ronson in a boxing ring in the sky Disch found "the telltale scent of skepticism that every vigilante will recognize as a mark of the

Secular Humanist." One would think that this reviewer might at least have noticed Cassie's more conventional religious dedication. "Secular Humanist" is an amusingly mistaken label for the man who may be, in an enlightened sense, the best Christian novelist in American today. Disch also complained that "it is hard to take the book's treatment of medical ethics, or lack thereof, very seriously." In this he is right. It should be obvious that the question of "medical ethics" is a red herring in the novel.[4]

This review troubled Cormier a little, not for the judgment on himself but because it worried him that he might have arbitrarily denied his characters the comfort of visits from clergymen. "It would have been very easily done, to have a priest come in on Thursday and be sitting with Mazzo," he mused, "and have Barney walk by and see a priest with him to give a little bit of solace. Or Allie Roon, who might have been Protestant, to have a minister there." But that would mean acknowledging that the world outside was aware and concerned: "the families would be dropping in . . . and the do-gooders would be stopping by with fruit—" and then the Complex is no longer an island apart—the literary frame is gone.

"Free choice, the Handyman said, you have free choice here. A laugh, of course," thinks Barney. Yet, outside the terrible, implacable fact of impending death, they do have free choice, and the other characters have used it. Billy the Kidney and Allie Roon have chosen to come to the Complex so that their deaths might help others, and although they are embarrassed to talk about it, the commitment does give each of them some spiritual comfort. Mazzo has made the choice for the wrong reasons—to die more quickly—and finds only selfish anger in it. Faith has no reality for him. Cassie's attraction to total spiritual surrender he sees only as a passing fad. Barney, too, has made the choice, but he doesn't know it. The decision to commit himself to the Complex happened in the immediate past that has been erased from his mind. So Barney must find elsewhere that humanizing gesture against the Implacable that is so central in Cormier's cosmos.

Before he can act he must find out who he is. Or perhaps the other way around, as the existentialists would have it. Through action we make our own meaning for our existence. Cassie's first words to Barney are, "I know who you are." But *he* doesn't. Just before the terrifying experiment in which his identity is to be entirely obliterated, he writes down what he knows about himself: his name, his age, his weight, his height. That is all. In childhood memory (perhaps a manufactured memory) he recalls losing his mother in a department store. "I started to scream, not only because I had lost my mother but because I didn't know who I was. Without my mother to verify who I was, I was lost." Yet the experiment he is about to undergo is terror beyond that terror because, as the Handyman explains in a misguided attempt at comfort, "you will not remember your name. But consider this: You will also not remember not knowing your name." He is given the drug, and awakes in a room that is the classic existential place between worlds: bare, hard chairs lined up against the walls, coffee table with magazines, flat calendar art on the wall—a waiting room for hell. "He was alone, cast adrift, lost, unrelated to anything." A face appears on a television screen and asks him, in the fairy-tale manner, the obligatory three questions. They take the form of word associations. "Snow," "car"—before the third question can be asked, Barney in a panic finds it for himself. *Who am I*? and then *What am I*? He can find no answer. Here, in the existential dilemma, Cormier's preoccupation with identity is laid bare.

But all the while through his labor on the Bumblebee Barney has been finding the answer without being aware he was seeking it. At the moment that he, screwdriver in hand, stands ready to being disassembling the car, he has an impulse to say a prayer. Then, in a moment that blares out the triumphant Richard Strauss theme from the film *2001*, "he tossed the screwdriver into the air, watched it tumbling and turning and falling, caught it with a hand that was marvelously ready and waiting. And he began to take the car apart."

Like all of us, Barney thinks he is the only one who is not going to die. Even before, the Handyman tells him, in the other hospital, he had not come to the stage of acceptance as others did. When he is finally, undeniably confronted with the fact of his mortality, the Bumblebee, which began as an attempt to transform his nightmare of the rainy car, is itself transformed. Now it becomes a defiant affirmation, "a shared vision of freedom and rebirth." When Barney first gazes down from the skylight in the attic he sees only the junkyard, rows of bleak tenements, an old cemetery "with tombstones like small teeth scattered on a rug." But when he stands with Mazzo and Billy on the threshold of the flight, the view, like his soul, is transfigured—"the sweep of sky spinning with stars, the moon radiating silver, turning the sloping roof into a glittering ski slide, the lights of Monument center glowing in the distance, staining the sky with gold." At the last minute he realizes that suicide is irreconcilable with an act of faith. The Bumblebee soars, and in this supremely irrational gesture is ultimate hope. "All stories, if continued far enough, end in death," said Ernest Hemingway.[5] But perhaps, just perhaps, he was wrong.

11. *Fade*

What if . . . you could make yourself invisible? What would you do first? How would this ability change your life and your world? What would be its pleasures and dangers? Would it be a gift or a curse?

A suitable subject for science fiction writers. Yet in 1988 Cormier, who had built a firm reputation on realism, on his ability to look even the grimmest facts straight in the eye, wrote a novel about a boy who could make himself invisible. It is apparent that Cormier delights in jolting his readers with the unexpected, and he has confessed his fear of repeating himself,[1] so it is not really so surprising that after *Beyond the Chocolate War* had rounded off the group of four dark young adult novels that began with *The Chocolate War* he should veer off in a new direction. But while Cormier moved toward science fiction, the story remains firmly rooted in reality, even autobiography. Characteristically, he has used the idea of invisibility to explore the intersection of truth and fiction and the nature of belief and guilt, while telling a fast-moving and suspenseful tale dusted with the poignancy of adolescent first love. "Imagine what might happen if Holden Caulfield stepped into H. G. Wells's classic science fiction novel, *The Invisible Man*," Stephen King has said about *Fade*.[2] Or if Anthony Michael Hall took on the Claude Rains role in the 1933 film based on that book?

The idea of invisibility has always been a part of human folklore. To be unseen is an inherent quality of the gods, as it is of spirits and the dead. In some folk beliefs, the gods and heroes possessed garments such as a cloak or a helmet or a cap that could cause the wearer to vanish, and the Greek gods could make a favorite human disappear suddenly to escape pursuit or danger. In some cultures mortals with superior mystic knowledge like shamans and witches were believed to be able to invoke invisibility as a power or a protection by means of magical potions, ointments, or spells.[3] In the Christian tradition, God is the All-Seeing Unseen, and Jesus Christ is God made visible through the Incarnation. Modern metaphysical systems like theosophy postulate an astral body, and many people claim to have had out-of-body experiences in which an invisible form of the self goes a-journeying.

Given the universality of the concept, then, it is puzzling how seldom it appears in modern literature. Apart from an occasional science fiction short story, *The Invisible Man* stood alone until very recently. (Ralph Ellison's novel, *Invisible Man*, of course, uses the term as a metaphor for racism.) In Wells's story, an irascible scientist accidentally renders himself invisible during an experiment and is unable to reverse the transformation in spite of his frantic efforts to find an antidote. Raging through the streets of the country village where he has come to find solitude for his experiments, he is eventually undone by his own violence.[4]

Thinking he had the field all to himself, Cormier was immersed in the writing of *Fade* in 1987, when, one Sunday, he opened the *New York Times* and found, much to his consternation, reviews of not one, but two new novels built around the idea: *Being Invisible* by Thomas Berger and *Memoirs of an Invisible Man* by H. F. Saint. Marilyn Marlow assured him that there was no cause for alarm because the treatments were entirely different, and this proved to be true. Berger has written a glib sexual farce in which an invisible man uses his ability as a device to avoid inconvenience or embarrassment. He follows along on his ex-wife's date, leaves restaurants and taxis without paying, and gets out of awkward bedroom liaisons by vanishing.[5] Saint's novel is a prolonged chase, a suspense story in which a man who has been made incorporeal by a nuclear accident attempts to elude the scientists and government agents who would use him for their own purposes. The interest lies in watching the ingenuity with which he overcomes the problems and puzzles that invisibility puts in the way of his desperate escape.[6] Although *Memoirs* was on best-seller lists for several weeks, neither book proved memorable in the long run, and by the time *Fade* was published more than a year later the coincidence was not an issue.

However, it is interesting to compare these three predecessors to *Fade* in their interpretations of the mechanics and literary conventions of the state of invisibility. Both Wells's and Saint's protagonists are stuck in their altered state (hence their respective fury and panic), but Berger's man can turn it on and off by an exercise of will. Cormier's Paul Moreaux is in both situations: he can choose to go in and out of the fade but it also comes on him by itself.

What about clothes—what does an invisible man wear, and can other people see it? Wells's man makes himself visible and somewhat socially acceptable with a suit, a hat, a wig, dark glasses, facial bandages, and a false nose (Saint's protagonist goes to a Halloween party dressed like him), but he must go naked to be unseen. The nuclear mishap that rendered Saint's man incorporeal has also made a whole building and its contents disappear, so that the clothes he is wearing and any that he can salvage from the site are invisible, but anything he dons (or picks up) from the outside world can be seen. Berger's protagonist discovers that everything he touches instantly vanishes. Cormier establishes that garments and objects within the immediate energy of Paul's flesh cannot be seen, although anything extra he holds (like a knife) can. The consumption of food is governed by the same rules—visible until absorbed into the body—and Saint's fugitive watches his own digestive processes with horrid fascination. Eyelids, too, are transparent to their owners in all four books, and Wells adds the detail that the dead tips of fingernails and a stain on the finger remain when the hand has disappeared.

All have trouble at first balancing and stepping with feet they cannot see, and when they walk in the streets they are jostled and rammed. "People kept coming and going in a space which, unless they saw someone else in the way, they assumed was theirs to occupy exclusively," says Berger.[7] (Paul alone is free of this hazard on the uncrowded streets of Monument.) Wells's chilly experimenter finds that snow, fog, rain, and dust make his outline appear, and Saint adds soapsuds to that list, but for neither Berger nor Cormier are these things revealing. Wells and Saint play with the dramatic possibilities of bodiless footprints in snow or on grass and rugs.

Detection by dogs is a very Cormier-like worry, and sure enough, in the last section of *Fade* Ozzie is approached by a growling but puzzled German shepherd. Wells's mad scientist realizes "the nose is to the mind of a dog what the eye is to the mind of a seeing man,"[8] but Saint's protagonist is relieved to find that he is as unsensed by the guard dogs' noses as he is by their eyes. Cormier adds one more item to this list of variable rules governing literary incorporeality: Paul, even in his visible state, cannot be photographed, and the avoidance of cameras becomes a serious limitation on his later life.

None of these three novels directly influenced the writing of *Fade*, simply because Cormier deliberately did not read them. But the 1933 film *The Invisible Man* was indeed a part of the book's genesis. Based on the Wells novel, the film was directed by James Whale of *Frankenstein* fame and starred Claude Rains.[9] Few people who have seen this movie will ever forget the scene in which Rains slowly unwinds his head bandages to reveal a gaping nothing. Cormier was mightily impressed by the film as a boy, and confesses to still enjoying it on video. Paul refers to it several times in *Fade*, once, when a boy, as "the movie where the man wrapped himself in bandages." Later Jules credits it with the genesis of the manuscript. Other lighthearted invisibility films of the era that Cormier might remember include *Topper* and *Blithe Spirit*, in which people who have died return to wreak mischief on their survivors.

A literary influence that Cormier himself credits is Graham Greene's *The End of the Affair*, in which someone, like Paul's agent Meredith, "knows the truth but is trying to disprove it all the time." It may or may not be significant that in late 1986 Cormier wrote an admiring review for the *Los Angeles Times* on *The Flight of the Cassowary* by John LeVert, a book in which a boy named Paul is living an ordinary teenage life when he discovers that he has an unexplained, unexpected supernatural ability that disturbs the course of his life.[10] That this Paul can become an animal and fly, not vanish, makes the coincidence no less intriguing.

And finally there is the question of the effect of the writing of Stephen King on *Fade*. The two writers are friendly acquaintances who enjoy one another's books. Cormier has said, "Stephen King lurked in the background. . . . Yet, I wasn't trying to write a Stephen King novel."[11] Certain details—the single eye that stares out of the old man's smashed head, the voice that tempts Ozzie from the fade, the violence of the knife fight—evoke King's melodramatic and bloody excesses. The breathless rhythm of the last section as the voices of Paul and Ozzie alternate more and more quickly is reminiscent of King at his best. Yet in context these passages are pure Cormier, the violence justified by the necessities of character and plot. King himself has praised the novel extravagantly: "I was absolutely riveted. . . . An exciting, fast-paced read . . . moving and enthralling. Cormier has always been a fine novelist, but *Fade* is easily his best work."[12]

Yet this novel that ends with such drama begins quietly as if it were going to be the nostalgic adventures of a French-Canadian–American Tom Sawyer. The time is 1938, and Paul Moreaux is thirteen. He lives in the Frenchtown section of Monument with his parents and his older brother, Armand, his younger brother, Bernard, and his twin sisters, Yvonne and Yvette. His best friend, Pete Lagniard, is just downstairs, and nearby are the houses of his grandparents and his many aunts and uncles. The life of this close French-Canadian community revolves around St. Jude's Church and the comb factory where most of the adults go to work each day.

Paul is a shy, secretive boy who yearns to be a writer. Although he is happy growing up in this warm family environment, he longs for adventure in the distant places of the globe. This longing is personified for him by his uncle Adelard, a wanderer who returns only occasionally and who is the subject of a mysterious anecdote. Long ago a photograph had been taken of the whole family, but when the picture was developed, in the place where Adelard had been standing was only a blank space. Paul is obsessed by this story, and questions his father about it whenever he gets a chance. In the meantime, however, another wanderer returns, Paul's voluptuous Aunt Rosanna. Paul falls instantly in love, and she teases him with affectionate flirtatiousness.

One night Paul and Pete spy on a meeting of the Ku Klux Klan at Moccasin Pond and find themselves caught in the midst of a brawl when the angry Frenchtown locals arrive. Fleeing, Paul unexplainedly escapes the notice of the burly Klansman who is pursuing him. As the summer wears on, he secretly follows and eavesdrops on his aunt, and one day surprises her alone in her room. Getting up his courage, he gives her a love poem he has written, but then is inflamed by her beauty to a sexual climax, and runs off in mortification. His troubles increase when he is chased by the bully Omer LaBatt, but again he mysteriously escapes his pursuer's notice. He continues to shadow Rosanna, and follows her to the apartment of the town villain, Rudolphe Toubert. When she emerges she leads him to a secluded picnic area by the river, where she confides in him that Toubert fathered her child, which was born dead several years before. In the intimacy of the conversation, she guides Paul's hand to her breast, and suddenly he realizes that love is more than physical desire. Later, when she leaves town abruptly he continues to feel longing and guilt, even though she has left him an affectionate (and misspelled) note of farewell.

Adelard returns, and Paul is flattered to notice that his uncle seems to seek out his company. One rainy afternoon he finds Paul home alone and takes the opportunity to reveal to him the secret that has passed from uncle to nephew for generations. Adelard can make himself "fade," or become invisible, and Paul, who has half suspected it by now, also has the ability. Adelard instructs him in the painful transition technique and charges him never to tell a living soul. Dazzled by his new power, Paul begins to experiment with its possibilities. He invisibly watches Pete and his friends on the street corner and then follows a young girl into the back room of Dondier's Market, where he is stunned and repelled to see the elderly grocer pay her to allow him to perform cunnilingus on her skinny adolescent body.

Paul tries to confess this voyeurism and his dalliance with Rosanna to the priest, but is unable to ask whether the fade is a sin. He finds that it is beginning to set him apart from the rest of his world—and from God. His uneasiness is confirmed when Adelard, before leaving once more, tells him that the fade has been a burden to him and that he blames it and himself for the long-ago death of his younger brother, Vincent. He warns Paul always to use the power for good and speculates on the terrible possibilities of a future evil fader.

School begins, and Paul and his cousin Jules are plunged into the new world of Silas B. Thornton Junior High School. At first he is delighted by the new opportunities, but when a teacher savagely disparages a story he has written, he realizes that these advantages are not for boys who come from Frenchtown. Unexpectedly, he is befriended by cool, wealthy Emerson Winslow who takes him home after school and introduces him to his twin sister, Page, as "a writer." Paul is entranced by the twins' beauty and sophistication and returns that night in the fade, only to become a shocked and unwilling witness to an incestuous sexual encounter between the pair. When he finds Omer LaBatt persecuting a younger boy in an alley and drives him off with unnecessarily vicious invisible kicks and blows, he is appalled to notice that this time the fade has come uninvited and that it has brought no good to his life.

Meanwhile, the workers' growing dissatisfaction with conditions at the comb factory results in a strike. Rudolphe Toubert is instrumental in arranging to have scabs brought in, and with their arrival a fight breaks out on the picket lines. Paul's father is stabbed, and in horror Paul runs away, invites the fade, and goes invisibly to the office of Toubert to revenge his father and his aunt. He picks up a knife . . .

When he returns home, he learns that his father has survived.

Toubert is found dead, but the murder is blamed on Toubert's missing henchman, not Paul. Three weeks later Paul's younger brother, Bernard, like his Uncle Vincent a generation before, dies suddenly in his sleep.

At this point the narrative breaks off, and a new voice begins. The time has shifted to 1988, and Susan Roget, a distant relative of the famous but reclusive writer Paul Roget, explains that she has come to New York to work as an assistant in the office of Paul's former agent Meredith Martin, and to live with her for the summer in her Greenwich Village apartment. Paul has died in 1967, before Susan was born, but his career has been an important influence on her life and her ambition to become a writer. Snooping through Meredith's closets one day when the agent is out, Susan comes upon a hidden manuscript that turns out to be the Frenchtown story we have just read.

Susan is stunned, and when she confesses her find to Meredith, she finds that the older woman is deeply troubled by the possibly autobiographical nature of the narrative. Paul has always given his stories Frenchtown settings, but in this case he has used actual people and events, named real names. If the rest of the story is real, then so is the fade—and maybe Paul is also a murderer, although his words are inconclusive on this point.

Meredith is ambivalent, and so has sent the manuscript to Jules, Susan's grandfather, for a confidential opinion. She shows Susan the report Jules has written. While trying to deny the autobiographical nature of the narrative and to prove that the story, and the fade, are fiction, Jules inadvertently confirms that the characters and major events are indeed real. Confused and upset, Susan tries to push away the idea that Paul could actually make himself invisible. But Meredith shows her a piece of convincing evidence, a series of three photographs taken secretly by a friend of hers in which Paul is first a blur, and then not there at all. In the morning Susan finds that Meredith has left her a note of apology and a second part of the manuscript, whose existence she had previously kept a secret from Susan.

Paul's adult voice resumes the tale, as Susan reads what he has written. It is now 1963. Paul has become a distinguished novelist, but still lives on the top floor of a Frenchtown three-decker opposite St. Jude's Church. His brothers and sisters have married and had children, and Paul has cultivated the company of his nieces and nephews, watching for the next fader, although thus far he has been unable to detect signs of the fade in any of his nephews. Although he has vowed never to invoke the fade again, it comes on him unexpectedly more and more often, and he lives in dread of detection. This fear has kept him a recluse, afraid to travel, to reap the public rewards of his success, even to seek medical help when he is ill. Like Adelard, he finds that the fade has diminished him over the years. Paul now confesses that he did kill Toubert, describing the events of that night. Bernard's death seemed to him to be a retribution for his sin, even though Adelard explained to him at the wake that the fade had had little to do with the equivalent death of Vincent. Paul has sought forgiveness from God in vain, and voices torture him with guilt in the night. When his sister Rose confides that she once gave birth to an illegitimate child and left it for adoption in a convent in Maine, he knows that he has found the next fader at last. To go to him and counsel him is Paul's only route to salvation.

Here Ozzie, Rose's abandoned child, takes up the story in the third person. Now thirteen, he has lived a life of neglect and abuse. His alcoholic adoptive mother has died, and his brutal stepfather has beaten him so badly and so often that his nose is now a hideously deformed mass. For a time he ran away to the streets, where his only friend was the wino Old Man Pinder, but now he has been rescued by the nuns and lives in the convent near the town of Ramsey. He is full of rage at the world, and when the fade finds him, he knows just what to do. He goes directly to his stepfather and beats his head to a pulp with a hammer. Delirious with his new power, he goes on an invisible rampage of hitting and breaking, and soon he finds a voice in his head is urging him to do even worse things, even to suspect the kindness of the nun who has cared for him. When Old Man Pinder accidentally discovers his secret, the voice tells Ozzie to kill him and then to also silence the nun. Ozzie resists temporarily, but when he finds Old Man Pinder has become an informant to Paul, the stranger who has been asking about him, Ozzie beats the old wino's skull in with a rock. The dying old man drags himself to Paul to warn him to save the nun. In a midnight courtyard in Ramsey, the two faders meet for a showdown. Paul tries to offer compassion and help, but the voice in Ozzie's head understands only suspicion and violence. A knife fight between the two invisibles ends with Paul committing a second, but necessary, murder.

In an epilogue, Susan and Meredith try to convince themselves that the story is fiction. The fade, of course, is obviously impossible, they agree without conviction, and Meredith decides to publish the manuscript. Susan, however, remembers (but doesn't mention to Meredith) a crucial piece of information told her by Jules, a piece of information he omitted from his report to Meredith. When he and Paul were boys, one afternoon in the public library Paul disappeared in the stacks and Jules could not find him for an hour. For Susan this is evidence of the reality of the fade, and when she stumbles on a newspaper story about a series of mysterious vandalisms in a nearby state, she begins to realize that there may be a new fader, and her knowledge and her obligation to Paul may have given her a responsibility that terrifies her.

The literary style of *Fade*, especially in the first section, is deceptively simple and straightforward. There is none of the complex layering, the brilliant metaphors and allusions that typify Cormier's other novels. Only when one attempts to summarize the story does it become clear how intricately linked are the multitude of apparently rambling events. There are thirty-three developed characters (and fifty-five more who are mentioned by name), and each has an essential part in the progress of the plot. Even the seemingly self-indulgent autobiographical details of Frenchtown life are integral in developing the borderless interweave of reality and fiction that makes the novel so disturbing.

Only very occasionally is the careful reader aware of Cormier exercising his stylistic powers. There are a number of doublings, or repeated but contrasted patterns: two illegitimate births (to Rose and to Rosanna), two young brothers suddenly dead (Vincent and Bernard), two bullies (Bull Zimmer and Omer LaBatt), two sets of twins (Yvonne and Yvette, and Emerson and Page), two teenage boys working in grocery stores (Paul and Ozzie), two brawls (the Ku Klux Klan and the strikers), two exiled wanderers (Adelard and Rosanna), and two deaths by knifing (Toubert and Ozzie). Paul himself remarks some of these: "The endless, unceasing repetitions. The tides of life and living."

Even more striking is the way in which Cormier introduces ideas and words referring to invisibility and secrecy long before he has revealed the fade. The first thing we learn about Adelard is that "he was always disappearing," meaning, in this context, that he was always going away on a journey. "It's hard to see what isn't there," says Louis Moreaux jokingly. Paul feels different and alienated before he has a reason to, and ironically he longs for a life of drama and mystery. He often behaves as if he were invisible before he can be, searching Rosanna's room and shadowing her in the street. He loves secrets, and prides himself on the ability to hide, which he uses to escape Omer before he finds that there is a better way. The Ku Klux Klan are "invisible" within their hoods, "their eyes dark caves." And when Adelard comes to the tenement to reveal the secret to Paul on that fateful rainy afternoon, his footsteps cross the piazza and pause at the bottom of the steps as if he were already disembodied.

A playful stylistic conceit is the suggestion of the bully Omer LaBatt as a hostile dog. In his dumb, unreasoned animosity, he stands silently barring the path, confronting, sometimes chasing, sometimes only standing his ground. He has pale yellow eyes and "a vicious grin that revealed jagged teeth" and "trying to approach Omer LaBatt to make some kind of peace would be like coming face-to-face with an animal."

Other characterizations are more human. Adelard is one of the most poignant actors in this intricate drama. Even as a young man his clothes and his eyes are pale and faded, a forerunner of the effect the fade is to have on his soul. He knows he is utterly trapped by his destiny, yet there is a wry gallantry about him. "He has a reputation for avoiding straight answers," yet he smiles and changes the subject with gentle humor when questioned too closely on sensitive matters like the mysterious photograph.

Later, he takes on a tragic dimension under the burden of the fade, "the lines of weariness enclosing his mouth, the dark pouches like bruises under his eyes." When he confesses to Paul that the fade has driven him to theft and near-rape, he thinks of himself as a monster. But for Paul he will always be "the only person who had the dimensions of a hero, who dared to be different, who wandered the earth."

The other wanderer, Rosanna, is one of Cormier's most endearing feminine creations. Through Paul's eyes, she is that familiar Cormier woman, the utterly desirable and completely unattainable love object. But we suspect that she is a bit of a slut, and Jules later confirms it. Rosanna is good-hearted, affectionate, but lazy and not too bright. Her fatal flaw is that she is unable to resist the temptation to exercise her one avenue to power. She is seduced by seduction and gets carried away every time, even approaching incest with her nephew. But she means well always, and the reader, like Paul, can't help being fond of her.

The twins, Emerson and Page Winslow, echo Cassie and Mazzo from *Bumblebee* in their secret link, although the latter pair are not incestuous. Emerson's name is one of the very few in *Fade* that has an allusive level. In its reference to the poet and the painter (Ralph Waldo Emerson and Winslow Homer) it is a name that evokes the noblest of American culture. By describing Emerson and Page as identical halves of a whole that must inevitably come together, Cormier has made the revelation of their union a bit less shocking. They are "reflections embracing each other, blending together," and it seems quite appropriate that Emerson should finish his life in a monastery after Page's death.

Other figures in the cast of *Fade* recall people in earlier Cormier novels. He himself has described Susan, Amy Hertz, and Cassie all as "the rowdy young woman with hidden depths."[13] Shy, fearful Adam of *I Am the Cheese* (whose real name is Paul) is in some respects like our Frenchtown fader. Cormier has compared Ozzie with Archie Costello of *The Chocolate War*,[14] but on closer inspection they are alike only in their penchant for evil-doing. Archie is elegant, intelligent, and his evil is pure and unexplained.

Ozzie, as an angry victim of society, is all too understandable in his need to get even, and his mind is crude and dull. The ending of *Fade* recalls the last lines of *Beyond the Chocolate War* and *After the First Death*. Like Archie, like Miro, the new fader has served an apprenticeship in evil and is now about to launch unspeakable destruction on the adult world.

Cormier has said that *Fade* is "probably the most autobiographical novel I've ever written—not the facts of my life but the background. . . . I was expanding on my childhood days—sort of reliving my childhood."[15] As we have seen, all of his books are set in the imaginary town of Monument, which is closely modeled on the real towns of Leominster and Fitchburg; significant fictional events in his books often are set in real places, and he has used his French Hill childhood in his short stories. But *Fade* goes beyond this: there are extended passages drawn from Cormier's early memories or cannibalized from his first novel, *Act of Contrition*. The wake, the Rub Room (the awful basement room at the comb factory to which Paul's father is demoted), the chorus of factory whistles, the night sounds in the crowded bedroom—all are part of his past life. Moccasin Pond is Fort Pond; Ransom Hill is Rice Hill; Silas B. Thornton Junior High School is May A. Gallagher Junior High School; Ramsey is the hamlet of Ayer near Fort Devens; and the Plymouth Theater actually existed until it was torn down several years ago. Even the mysterious photograph was real, and the source of the "what if?" for the novel. Devotees of Cormieriana are apt to feel as Susan did on discovering the Frenchtown manuscript: "I have devoured every piece of material about him and here was new, exciting stuff."

Another kind of childhood memory that has crept into *Fade* is the many conscious echoes from the movies of the thirties. The searchlights sweep over Paul's head at the KKK rally as if he were James Cagney breaking out of the pen; he tosses a stone to divert the butler at the door of the Winslow house; Le Farge the gravedigger is pure Boris Karloff; Louis Moreaux in the Rub Room is "like a slave in a horror film" to his son's eyes; Emerson with his scarf reminds him of a gallant British flier in the Great War;

the knife that kills Ozzie descends with excruciating and formulaic slowness, and Ramsey is the definitive arcaded cowboy town.

In this seamless blend of autobiography, fiction, and remembered fiction it is important to keep one's bearings by holding firmly to the fact that it is the settings, not the characters or events, that are real. Although Cormier did have a best friend named Pete who lived downstairs, although he did have twin siblings and a brother who died young, none of the *Fade* uncles resembles his own, who, like his father, were gentle men who would never think of rebelling against their employers. And although it is tempting, because of the matching alliteration, to equate Cormier's agent Marilyn Marlow with Paul's agent Meredith Martin, the personalities of the two women are quite different, and it is Anita Silvey of *Horn Book*, not Marilyn Marlow, who is famous for her collection of hats.

Jules speaks of "the tricky mirror of memory—making it difficult to separate the real from the unreal," and Cormier has deliberately used this trick mirror to fuddle our perceptions. Paul says, "I have fictionalized so much of what happened in those days that sometimes, rereading my books and thinking of the past, I'm not sure what's real and what isn't." Cormier himself has exactly the same problem, he admitted in the essay for *Horn Book* published just before *Fade*.[16] His motives in evoking his childhood so literally were not so much nostalgia, he has explained, as deliberate technique. "I wanted to make something impossible seem possible, by rooting it in autobiography to make it real." The curious trick, the element that makes the reader's head buzz, is that Cormier's autobiography is also Paul's autobiography, and on its reality turns the question of whether the fade is real. Paul Roget was thirteen in Frenchtown in 1938, and so was his creation Paul Moreaux, and so was his creator Robert Cormier. He has made Paul as a writer parallel himself as a writer, including such well-known Cormierisms as a devotion to "what if." Like Paul, Cormier follows "his usual method of placing a fictional story against a very real background"—but not always. As Meredith says of Paul, he "has written his most realistic, autobiographical novel yet. And if he wrote it that way, then he wanted us to believe what happened in the novel. And we must believe all of it or none of it." And Susan answers dubiously, "Maybe Paul had to create a real world so that the reader would be *forced* to believe the fantasy. But that doesn't mean the fantasy was real." So compelling is this monkey puzzle of truth and fiction that in the first few months after *Fade*'s publication one friend after another would take Cormier aside confidentially and ask with hesitant intensity, "Bob, *can* you fade?"

The book exerted a compelling force over Cormier, too, during its composition. "It just consumed me," he says, and he let himself go as never before. The first version was 600 pages long. At this time, Cormier had just ended his lifetime publishing association with Pantheon and had signed new contracts with Delacorte Press. The move was amicable, but not without emotion for Cormier. His longtime editor Fabio Cohen had left Pantheon after *Eight Plus One*, and although Cormier worked well with editors Pat Ross on *Bumblebee* and Dinah Stevenson on *Beyond the Chocolate War*, he felt it was time for a change.

At Delacorte he and Olga Litowinsky worked together to edit the giant manuscript down to a workable size. Cormier's affection for the material had led him to write many irrelevant scenes and characters. Paul had a second younger brother, Roger, who was the smart-aleck genius of the family. His uncle Edgar had a large role in the union scenes; the young woman who tries to photograph Paul ran away with a whole chapter; the seventeenth-century fader from France was attacked by pirates while crossing to America. Even after the manuscript was typeset to galleys he continued to write obsessively—Susan at Jules's funeral, Rosanna as an old lady, and so on.

Other passages and characters underwent drastic changes. Originally Ozzie was a monster and his killings were extremely bloody. But recognizing that it was "Stephen King stuff," Cormier went back and humanized the character and toned down the violence. Originally, too, Paul died in a mental institution, and Meredith, visiting, was told of two instances where he had disappeared from his room. Cormier played with the idea of making

Rosanna's baby survive to become the next fader, but then realized that the relationship was wrong.

The most important change involved the structure. The middle section in early versions was entirely in Jules's voice. The stodginess of his personality bothered Cormier, and an uneasy sense that it just wasn't working. After some thought Litowinsky suggested that a new character might carry the action, perhaps a young woman. Cormier loved the idea, and "Susan was full blown within twenty-four hours." It was also a canny marketing decision on Litowinsky's part to add another teenage voice to what was becoming a rather adult novel.

Another editorial suggestion, but one that Cormier resisted, was the removal of the Winslow twins. Litowinsky felt that they added nothing to the story and was perhaps uncomfortable with the incest scene. But Cormier felt that the characters served several important purposes: the contrast of their life of wealth and ease to Paul's own working-class background showed him the other side of life; Emerson was the first to respect him as a writer, and at their house the fade was again brought into play and again backfired. Cormier justifies the incest scene itself, as well as the other sexual scenes in the book, by pointing out that these experiences must shock Paul enough to make him realize that the fade is a curse—and what is shocking to Paul must necessarily be so to the reader. Actually, Paul turns and covers his ears after his first realization of what is happening. "I could have written a much more voluptuous scene," Cormier protests with accuracy. "I don't wallow in it. My conscience is clear. I could have made it much more graphic, and I didn't, really."

The fact remains that *Fade* is Robert Cormier's most sexually specific novel, but these scenes come directly out of Paul's character. He is a young boy on the verge of exploring adult sexuality, but with a penchant for voyeurism because he is by nature a shy observer. Quite early in the novel we see him setting a pattern of gratification from contemplating what is forbidden, as when he reaches orgasm from staring at Rosanna's breasts. His use of the fade fits into this pattern and he uses it to satisfy his desire to look all he wants and not be seen. Because he is by nature a sexual spy it is no accident that the fade leads him to "dark and nasty secrets it was better not to know about."

The structure of *Fade* bears some examination. Zena Sutherland, writing for the *Bulletin of the Center for Children's Books*, says, "*Fade* is brilliant in conception, intricate in structure."[16] From one perspective, it might be described as an unpublished novel interrupted in the middle by a discussion of its reality. In another perspective, Cormier sees it as two disparate halves: a nice, docile ethnic story, and then a sudden turning point that jolts it into another kind of story entirely.[17] (That crucial point, of course, is the moment when Paul turns toward Adelard on the rain-soaked balcony and sees that his uncle has vanished.)

The publisher breaks the book into three sections labeled "Paul," "Susan," and "Ozzie," although the voice in the second section is as much Jules's as Susan's, and the third section is not Ozzie speaking but Paul, writing both in the first and third person. These divisions are useful, however, in getting a grip on the construction of the novel. There are three separate and distinct parts, connected by the plot but each with its own form, style, characters, rhythm, and intention. The Frenchtown idyll is a gentle nostalgic coming-of-age story. The "Susan" section is a contemplative but brittle essay-with-dialogue on the expediency of reality. The last section is a horror fantasy tale that plunges along to a classic cornball shootout. These three are linked only by the events of the story, and by the central concept of the fade. It is a measure of Cormier's skill that he has pulled them smoothly together into one unified narrative.

In addition to the three formal divisions in the novel there is a sequence of several voices, each distinctive and clearly differentiated from the others. First there is Paul as a naive teenager in 1938, but the actual speaker is Paul the writer remembering his own young self. Then we hear Susan's bright, contemporary speech and Jules's stodgy and authoritative cadences. Next is the contrasting voice of Paul as a depressed adult, and then Ozzie's inarticulate and angry thoughts, but filtered through Paul's mind and pen. The last two switch back and forth with increasing frequency as the climax approaches, but there is never any doubt as to which is which. And last we return to an older and more responsible Susan. Technically, Cormier has pulled this off brilliantly, but for the reader, establishing so many new orientations to so many changes of speaker can be jarring—perhaps intentionally so. Zena Sutherland remarked, "The shifting of voice is not as successful here as in *I Am the Cheese*, seeming more obtrusively a literary device."[18]

The sheer number of people in Paul's big family can make it difficult for the reader to keep track of identities and relationships, but when the players are laid out in order a startling fact emerges. There can be no next fader because the line ends with Ozzie. The succession has always been from uncle to nephew. Since a nephew is the son of one's sibling, and Ozzie has no siblings, he therefore can be no one's uncle, even if he had lived —unless Rose had another child, who could then bear a son who would be the fader's nephew. Paul has written that Rose dies childless, but then, he didn't know about the first baby until she told him. Only Cormier knows for sure, and he won't tell. (Although he has confirmed that Jules was Victor's son.)

Another intriguing point revolves around the telling of Ozzie's story in the third person. How does Paul, who is the real speaker in this part, know what goes on in Ozzie's life and thoughts when he is not with him? Isn't it proof that he made up the whole thing, if he made up *some* things? At one point, Cormier had Susan raise this point hopefully but inconclusively with Meredith, but the passage was lost in subsequent cuts.

The struggles of Susan, Meredith, and Jules to believe, or not believe, in the truth of Paul's manuscript are cleverly designed to draw the reader into the same dilemma. Each has a very good reason for not wanting to accept the story as autobiography, aside from the disorienting prospect of invisibility as a real state. For Meredith, this potentially very profitable manuscript will be unpublishable unless she can convince herself it is fiction, because otherwise she will be in the position of besmirching the reputation of a respected writer and a dear friend (thus she sends only the first, least damaging, section to Jules for corroboration). For Jules, accepting the truth of the story is unthinkable (even though he

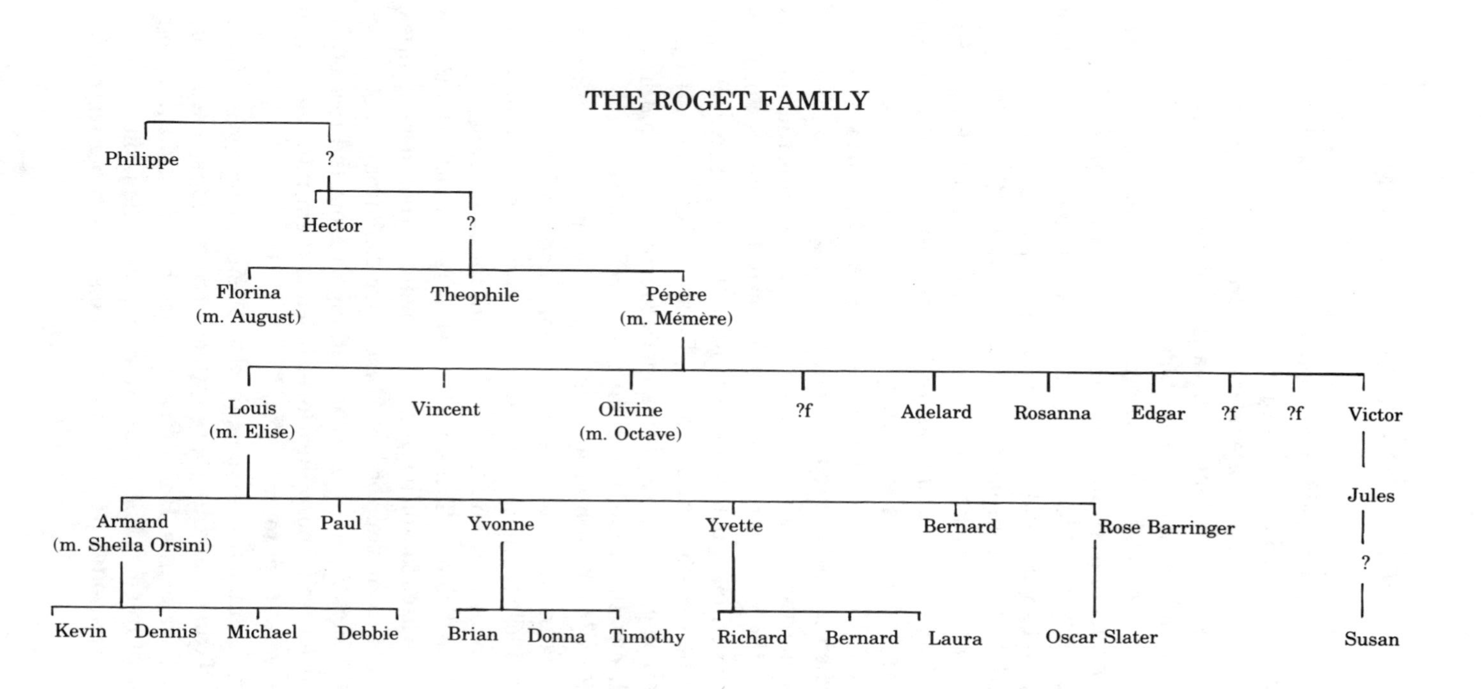
THE ROGET FAMILY
Philippe
?
Hector
?
Florina
(m. August)
Theophile
Pépère
(m. Mémère)
Louis
(m. Elise)
Vincent
Olivine
(m. Octave)
?f
Adelard
Rosanna
Edgar
?f
?f
Victor
Armand
(m. Sheila Orsini)
Paul
Yvonne
Yvette
Bernard
Rose Barringer
Jules
?
Kevin
Dennis
Michael
Debbie
Brian
Donna
Timothy
Richard
Bernard
Laura
Oscar Slater
Susan

holds a key piece of evidence) because then it will be known that the family has produced a murderer. For Susan (who is also withholding the same piece of evidence) there is a desperate need to think of the story as fantasy, because if it is true, it is she who must find and subdue the next fader.

Embedded in this section is a crafty piece of misdirection. When Susan begins to poke about in Meredith's apartment she tells us that she is "a terrible snoop." Aha, does she have Paul's love of secrecy and spying and has the fade made a gender jump? Later, Meredith looks her straight in the eye and says, "Fade." We think it is a command, just for one heartbeat, and so does Susan. Has Meredith suspected, and is she testing her? But no, with her next words we know it has all been a typical Cormier trick, and Meredith has only been asking her to consider the unreality of the term when it is presented in isolation.

A last question that must be pondered in analyzing this complex novel is the meaning of the fade. Clearly Cormier is speaking about something much more portentous than a fantasy technique for getting invisible. At one point, Delacorte had suggested that the book be called *The Fader*, a more concrete term that by contrast throws into relief the many subtle resonances of the actual title. "Fade" as a verb means not only "to vanish, disappear, become unseen" and "to lose color," but also "to lose freshness, wither; to lose strength or vitality; to decline in energy; to wane." In the movies it means "to dissolve into the next scene."

The fade has an effect on its possessors (its victims?) that is beyond the uses to which it is put. It consumes their personalities, their souls, even their bodies. "Like color gone from an old piece of cloth," says Adelard. It sets them apart from the rest of the world, even from those they love. It leads them into temptation and delivers them to evil.

At first Paul, like everyone, thinks invisibility brings unlimited power. "I can do anything, go anywhere, cross oceans, reach mountaintops," he exults. But almost at once he finds that the fade's promise of freedom is an illusion. Being invisible is only good for doing things you don't want anybody to see. In other words, bad things. The fade is useful solely for evil purposes, and so is inherently evil.

And inherently linked to guilt, he finds. For young Paul guilt means sex, and the fade is linked immediately to his incipient voyeuristic tendencies, as with Ozzie it connects with his potential for violence. There is a corrective function in being watched, and without it Paul has lost his moral compass. Soon he is a murderer, and finds that the fade has separated him even from the eyes of God. At the end, under the burden of being invisible to his Savior, he writes in despair, "Hell would not be anger but indifference."

The fade has its own purposes, its own voice that speaks in Paul's head and with Ozzie's mouth. The fade is an Other, as Paul understands when it throttles him with Ozzie's hands—"a deadly enemy, ageless, and mad." And implacable. The futile but redeeming act for Paul is a compassionate murder, as it was to have been for Barney. The real redemption from the curse of the fade comes from reaching out to teach and comfort the next one—as Adelard knew and Susan is soon to learn.

Several reviewers proposed that this was Robert Cormier's best novel yet. "Cormier has once again produced a profoundly disturbing, finely crafted gem that's hard, cold, and brilliant," said *Kirkus Reviews*.[19] "There is a sense of terror in daily life, the alien stranger loose out there and also lurking within, the fading of hope and trust," wrote Hazel Rochman in *Booklist*.[20] Cathi MacRae, in the *Wilson Library Bulletin*, called *Fade* "a paradigm for our use and abuse of power."[21] "Disturbing" was the most frequent verdict, and one that best pinpointed the feelings of many readers who found that after turning the last page of *Fade* it was impossible to keep from glancing nervously behind their chairs.

What next for Robert Cormier? Perhaps the nature of the critical reception of *Fade* points the way to a new direction. Although the book was edited and produced by Delacorte's Books for Young Readers Department, it was marketed from the adult side of the publishing house as well. Several journals, including the *San*

Francisco Chronicle, the *Washington Post Book World*, and the influential *New York Times Book Review* chose to judge it as a work for adults. After reminding readers of Cormier's early novels, Beverly Lyon Clark wrote (in the *New York Times*), "Now he has returned to writing for adults; at least that is how the new book is being published."[22] On the strength of the reviews, Dell planned to market the paperback among its top adult titles in the following season.

In other parts of the world Cormier has long had a strong readership among adults as well as teenagers. When he and Connie visited Paris in 1988 (where he claimed his Canadian French made them "fall down on the sidewalk laughing") he was surprised to find that the French translation of his works had brought him many grownup fans, and the audiences that appeared to hear him speak were often made up of people of all ages. In England, too, this was often the case, and when the Cormiers toured Australia in 1987 they found that his reputation had transcended the limits of young adult literature even Down Under.

But Robert Cormier at the typewriter has always followed the dictates of his soul, not the demands of the market or even of his readers. There are signs that he is chafing under the page limitations of the young adult novel: his last two manuscripts have needed severe editorial amputations to fit the size of the form. He has often yearned to write a nice tender love story, and lately he has speculated about following Archie Costello out into the world. But whatever comes next, we can be sure it will be a surprise. Perhaps his wife, Connie, who knows him better than anyone else, should have the last word. One day when she had been upstairs retyping a scene for him, she came down and stood in the doorway of his study, looking at him strangely.

"Who are you?" she said after a long moment. "We've been together all these years, but sometimes I wonder."[23]

Appendix

Films Based on Robert Cormier's Work

I Am the Cheese

Premier in Leominster, Massachusetts, 27 April 1983
Debut at Gemini Theater, New York City, 10 November 1983
Video distribution by Vestron

Cast:
- Adam—Robert Macnaughton
- Brint—Robert Wagner
- Adam's father—Don Murray
- Adam's mother—Hope Lange
- Amy—Cynthia Nixon
- Amy's father—Robert Cormier

Director—Robert Jiras

Producers—Robert Jiras and David Lange

Screenplay—Robert Jiras and David Lange

Cinematographer—David Quaid[1]

In spite of the dedicated involvement of top Hollywood talent, this film version of what is essentially a literary creation was a disaster. The cast included distinguished veteran actors Robert Wagner and Hope Lange, and Robert Macnaughton of *E.T.* fame. David Lange was the producer for *Klute* and *The Sterile Cuckoo* and Robert Jiras was executive producer for *The Boys in the Band*. Sound man Nat Boxer was the winner of an Academy Award for *Apocalypse Now*. For all these professionals the film was a labor of love. Hope Lange was quoted in the *Worcester Sunday Telegram* (18 July 1982) as saying, "This is one of the few times Hollywood people . . . have said, 'The hell with it. Let's just make a movie we believe in and that we're proud of working on.' "[2] Cormier himself was closely involved as a consultant in the production and the screenplay, and even played two brief scenes as Amy's newspaper editor father. Nevertheless, all this expertise and good intentions couldn't keep the film from looking and sounding amateurish. The photography is awkward and the acting, except for Macnaughton's work, is stiff and clumsy.

Perhaps some of the fault lies in the screenplay. In the pointless struggle to adapt a novel that depends on literary structure for its effect, the screenwriters made some unwise changes. Fat Arthur and Junior Varney were transformed into young hoods who confront Adam and steal his bike, giving an excuse for a chase sequence. Amy is no longer the tough, mischievous gamin who delights in The Numbers; for the movie audience she is just another pretty little girl. Brint is played by Robert Wagner as a grim but compassionate father substitute who hugs Adam when the going gets tough. And worst of all, a happy ending was pasted onto the plot, a final scene where Adam sneaks out of the hospital gate and sails off on his bike. Where would he go, and how many minutes would it be before They caught him again? It doesn't work, and it destroys the credibility of all that has gone before.

The film was withdrawn from commercial theaters after the New York critics lambasted it. Rex Reed summed up the problem when he wrote that *I Am the Cheese* was a book that never should have been touched.[3]

The Chocolate War

Premier in Los Angeles and New York, 28 October 1988, as a benefit for Amnesty International
Video distribution by Forum Home Video

Cast:
- Brother Leon—John Glover
- Jerry—Ilan Mitchell-Smith
- Archie—Wally Ward
- Obie—Doug Hutchinson
- Goober—Corey Gunnestad
- Emile Janza—Brent Fraser
- Brian Cochran—Robert Davenport
- Lisa—Jenny Wright
- Brother Jacques—Bud Cort
- Carter—Adam Baldwin
- Caroni—Ethan Sandler
- Gregory Bailey—Wayne Young
- Frank Bollo—Landon Wine
- Coach—Max Dixon

Jerry's Father—Roger Tompkins
Jerry's Mother—Elizabeth Yoffee
Brother Eugene—Robert Munns

Director—Keith Gordon

Producers—Jonathan D. Krane and Simon Lewis

Screenplay—Keith Gordon

Cinematographer—Tom Richmond

Art director—David Ensley[4]

For a time Robert Geller held the option for this most cinematic of Cormier's novels, and got as far as writing a screenplay.[5] An earlier option was held by a less than sensitive filmmaker who planned to turn Trinity into a girls' school where the major sport was competition roller skating. The raffle scene was to take place in a swimming pool, with wet t-shirts galore. Needless to say, Cormier was relieved when that option ran out. Fortunately, the film version that reached the screen was this sensitive and respectful treatment by Keith Gordon—although he also, like Robert Jiras, succumbed to the temptation to soften and brighten the ending to make it more palatable for a mass audience.

Previously, Keith Gordon had been best known for his role as the young owner of the diabolical car in the movie based on Stephen King's novel *Christine*. As a teenager he had been entranced by *I Am the Cheese* and had then sought out and read all Cormier's other books. For him the adapting and directing of *The Chocolate War* was the fulfillment of a longtime dream. He and the rest of the young cast and crew brought enthusiasm and dedication to the project, which allowed them to bring the film in under a minuscule budget of $700,000.[6]

One factor that made this possible was the serendipitous find of the abandoned St. Edward's Seminary near Seattle for the setting. This ecclesiastical building and its grounds had been given to the state as a public park, and its somber arch-windowed rooms stood empty, just waiting for the dark doings of the Vigils and Brother Leon.[7] Visually, the film captures the ominous atmosphere of the book perfectly with its gloomy halls, stark gray classrooms, and close blackness of the Vigils' basement meeting room. The electricity of Wally Ward's performance as Archie, with its subtlety and dark wit, saves the film from heaviness. John Glover, who had previously won critical praise for his role as a dying AIDS patient in NBC's *An Early Frost*,[8] is too tall and rangy to re-create the book's fleshy Brother Leon, but he manages to make him convincingly wicked nonetheless. Ilan Mitchell-Smith as Jerry is touchingly vulnerable, and, unfortunately, so is Brent Frazer as Emile Janza. By choosing to show inarticulate hurt and yearning for acceptance beneath Emile's bravado, Frazer has made the character more sympathetic and less malevolent, with damage to the story's structural balance.

The screenplay, written by Gordon himself, is fairly faithful to the literal events of the story and uses Cormier's dialogue almost word for word—until the last scene. After Archie draws the white marble, Carter demands that he draw once more, since two victims are involved, and this time the black marble appears when Archie opens his clenched fist. Jerry and Archie face each other in the boxing ring, and the first few raffle tickets allow Archie some vicious punches. Then Jerry gets one chance to hit back, and Archie responds with a low blow (an action as out of character for him as it is not for Janza, its literary perpetrator). Jerry reacts with a wild flurry that leaves Archie a bleeding mess on the floor. As the fickle crowd cheers and chants his name, Jerry at first is triumphant and then, when he sees Janza and Brother Leon applauding and a vision of his dead mother's sad face, he realizes that he has served the very system he tried to fight. "I should have sold the chocolates," he tells the Goober, as the lights fade. Later, we see Archie and Obie in the bleachers as in the opening scene, but now it is Obie in charge, and Archie, grimly humble, who must write down his chortling former henchman's vulgar and unsubtle ideas for assignments.

The film was widely reviewed; West Coast critics generally looked on it with favor, but New York cinema mavens were less kind. Most reviews acknowledged the film's literary origin, and several referred to the book as a "cult novel." Those who had read *The Chocolate War* often attempted to justify the new ending. Jack Lechner, in *American Film*, let the director himself explain it. "If the book's theme is 'you can't fight City Hall,'" said Gordon, "the film's theme is 'you've got to be careful when you're fighting City Hall that you're not doing exactly what City Hall wants you to do.'"

Notes and References

Chapter 2

1. Lee Grove, "Robert Cormier Comes of Age." *Boston Magazine*, December 1980, 78.

2. Richard R. Lingeman, "Boy in a Trap," *New York Times Book Review*, 22 May 1977, 51.

3. "From the Inside Out—the Author Speaks," in *Robert Cormier* [pamphlet] (New York, n.d.).

4. William A. Davis, "Tough Tales for Teenagers," *Boston Globe Magazine*, 16 November 1980, 17.

5. Geraldine De Luca and Roni Natov, "An Interview with Robert Cormier," *Lion and the Unicorn* 2 (Fall 1978):123.

6. Dolores Courtemanche, "Overnight Success—After 30 Years," *Worcester Sunday Telegram*, 18 July 1982, 11.

7. Tony Schwartz, "Teen-agers' Laureate," *Newsweek*, 16 July 1979, 87.

8. J. D. Salinger, *Catcher in the Rye* (Boston: Little, Brown, 1951), 25.

9. Davis, "Tough Tales," 22.

10. Anne Commire, ed., *Something about the Author* (Detroit: Gale, 1976), 10:28.

11. Ibid.

12. Davis, "Tough Tales," 12.

13. De Luca and Natov, "Interview with Robert Cormier," 120.

14. Robert Cormier, "Books Remembered," *The Calendar*, Children's Book Council, June/December 1986, unpaginated.

15. Ibid.

16. Ibid.

17. "From the Inside Out," 2.

18. Dolores Courtemanche, "Robert Cormier—in the Movies," *Worcester Sunday Telegram*, 18 July 1982, 9.

19. Ibid., 8.

20. Davis, "Tough Tales," 24.

21. Ibid., 26.
22. Ibid.
23. Ibid.
24. Frank McLaughlin, *Cheese, Chocolates, and Kids: A Day with Robert Cormier* (prepared for PBS, n.d.). Videotape. Robert E. Cormier Collection, Fitchburg State College, Fitchburg, Massachusetts.
25. Robert Cormier, *Eight Plus One: Stories* (New York: Pantheon, 1980), 45.
26. Commire, *Something about the Author*, 28.
27. Davis, "Tough Tales," 30.
28. Ibid.
29. Commire, *Something about the Author*, 28.
30. Judith Serebnick, "Triumph in Tragedy," *Library Journal*, 1 June 1960, 2203.
31. Phoebe-Lou Adams, review of *Now and at the Hour, Atlantic*, September 1960, 118.
32. Review of *Now and at the Hour, Time*, 1 August 1960, 68.
33. Davis, "Tough Tales," 32.
34. De Luca and Natov, "Interview with Robert Cormier," 112.
35. Cormier, *Eight Plus One*, vii.
36. Robert Cormier, Speech at Young Adult Services Division luncheon, American Library Association Conference, Dallas, Texas, 1979. Audiorecording.
37. De Luca and Natov, "Interview with Robert Cormier," 111.

Chapter 3

1. Robert Cormier [John Fitch IV, pseud.], "Staying Up Late—Comfort, Curse," column, *Fitchburg Sentinel*, 20 October 1970.
2. Donald R. Gallo, "Robert Cormier: The Author and the Man," *ALAN Review*, Fall 1981, 34.
3. McLaughlin, *Cheese, Chocolates, and Kids*.
4. Ibid.
5. Schwartz, "Teen-agers' Laureate," 92.
6. Robert Cormier, " 'Are You Working on a New Novel?' 'Yes.' " *ALAN Review*, Winter 1980, 31.
7. Paul Janeczco, "An Interview with Robert Cormier," *English Journal*, September 1977, 10.
8. Nicholas Basbanes, "Cormier Launches *Bumblebee*," *Worcester Evening Gazette*, 14 September 1983.
9. John Dinolfo, "Exclusive: An Interview with Robert Cormier," *You and Your World*, Teacher's Edition, part 2, 10 December 1980.

10. "Close-up: Robert Cormier, Novelist," *Fiction Writer's Market*, May 1983, 500.
11. Janeczco, "Interview with Robert Cormier."
12. De Luca and Natov, "Interview with Robert Cormier," 130.
13. Robert Cormier, "Forever Pedaling on the Road to Realism," in *Celebrating Children's Books: Essays on Children's Literature in Honor of Zena Sutherland*, ed. Betsy Hearne and Marilyn Kaye (New York: Lothrop, Lee & Shepard, 1981).
14. Cormier, " 'Are You Working on a New Novel?,' " 1.
15. McLaughlin, *Cheese, Chocolates, and Kids*.
16. Robert Cormier, "The Cormier Novels: The Cheerful Side of Controversy," *Catholic Library World*, July 1978, 6.
17. Laurel Graeber, "PW Interviews: Robert Cormier," *Publishers Weekly*, 7 October 1983, 98.
18. Cormier, "The Cheerful Side of Controversy," 6.
19. McLaughlin, *Cheese, Chocolates, and Kids*.
20. De Luca and Natov, "Interview with Robert Cormier," 116.
21. Cormier, "The Cheerful Side of Controversy."
22. Cormier, *Eight Plus One*, 60.
23. McLaughlin, *Cheese, Chocolates, and Kids*.
24. Dinolfo, "Exclusive," part 2.
25. Richard R. Lingeman, "Boy in a Trap," *New York Times Book Review*, 22 May 1977, 51.
26. James G. Lesniak, "Robert Cormier," In *Contemporary Authors*, New Revision Series (Detroit: Gale, 1981), 5:130.
27. Millicent Lenz, "A Romantic Ironist's Vision of Evil: Robert Cormier's *After the First Death*," paper presented at the Eighth Annual Conference of the Children's Literature Association, Minneapolis, Minnesota, March 1981.
28. Cormier, *Eight Plus One*, viii.
29. *Contemporary Literary Criticism* (Detroit: Gale, 1973), 12:133.
30. Davis, "Tough Tales," 35.
31. Lenz, "A Romantic Ironist's Vision."
32. Anne Scott MacLeod, "Robert Cormier and the Adolescent Novel," *Children's Literature in Education*, Summer 1981, 76.
33. De Luca and Natov, "Interview with Robert Cormier," 131.
34. George Christian, "Conversations: Novelist Robert Cormier and Reporter Nora Ephron," *Houston Chronicle*, 14 May 1978, 12.

Chapter 4

1. De Luca and Natov, "Interview with Robert Cormier," 134.

2. Bruce Clements, "A Second Look: *The Chocolate War*," *Horn Book*, April 1979, 217.
3. Betty Carter and Karen Harris, "Realism in Adolescent Fiction: In Defense of *The Chocolate War*," *Top of the News*, Spring 1980, 283.
4. Kenneth L. Donelson and Alleen Pace Nilsen, *Literature for Today's Young Adults* (Glenview, Ill.: Scott, Foresman, 1980), 186–89.
5. Alleen Pace Nilsen, "The Poetry of Naming in Young Adult Books," *ALAN Review*, Spring 1980, 3.
6. Cormier, "The Cheerful Side of Controversy," 6.
7. De Luca and Natov, "Interview with Robert Cormier," 122.
8. Renee Hoxie, letter, *Wilson Library Bulletin*, January 1982, 327.

Chapter 5

1. Betsy Hearne, "Whammo, You Lose," *Booklist*, July 1974, 1199.
2. Mary K. Chelton, review of *The Chocolate War*, *Library Journal*, 15 May 1974, 1480.
3. Richard Peck, "Delivering the Goods," *American Libraries*, October 1974, 492.
4. Theodore Weesner, review of *The Chocolate War*, *New York Times*, 5 May 1974, 15.
5. Review of *The Chocolate War*, *Publishers Weekly*, 15 April 1974, 52.
6. Review of *The Chocolate War*, *Junior Bookshelf*, June 1975, 194.
7. Martin Fagg, "Beasts and Monks," *New Statesman*, 23 May 1975, 694.
8. Peter Hunt, review of *The Chocolate War*, [London] *Times Literary Supplement*, 4 April 1975, 364.
9. Donelson and Nilsen, *Literature for Today's Young Adults*, 189.
10. Hunt, *Times Literary Supplement*, 364.
11. Gallo, "Robert Cormier," 33.
12. ". . . in Groton Social Studies Dept.," *Public Spirit* (Groton, Massachusetts), 16 September 1976, 1.
13. "Board Ends 'Chocolate War'; Students Support Book," *Fitchburg Sentinel-Enterprise*, 16 September 1976, 1.
14. Cormier, "The Cheerful Side of Controversy," 6.
15. Joy H. James, Judy Ingle, and Betsy Dyckes, letter to Dr. John Sprawls, principal, Irmo High School, Irmo, South Carolina, 1 May 1979. Robert E. Cormier Collection, Fitchburg State College, Fitchburg, Massachusetts.
16. Bobby Mather, "Parents Want Voice in School Book Choice,"

Lapeer County Press, 10 December 1980, 1.

17. Library Objection Form. Metamora Branch, Lapeer County Library System, Michigan, 28 October 1980. Robert E. Cormier Collection, Fitchburg State College, Fitchburg, Massachusetts.

18. "Vermont School Refuses to Censor Cormier Novel," *Fitchburg Sentinel-Enterprise*, 4 December 1981.

19. Peck, "Delivering the Goods," 492.

20. Schwartz, "Teen-agers' Laureate," 87.

21. Paulette Thompson, letter, "Books for Teens," *Newsweek*, 13 August 1979, 6.

22. Judith A. Duter, letter, "Books for Teens," *Newsweek*, 13 August 1979, 6.

23. Pelorus, review of *The Chocolate War, Signal*, September 1975, 146.

24. Norma Bagnall, "Realism: How Realistic Is It? A Look at *The Chocolate War*," *Top of the News*, Winter 1980, 214.

25. Carter and Harris, "Realism in Adolescent Fiction," 283.

26. Jay Daly, "The New Repression," *Top of the News*, Fall 1980, 79.

27. Elizabeth G. Knudsen, "Is There Hope for Young Adult Readers?" *Wilson Library Bulletin*, September 1981, 47.

28. Hoxie letter, *Wilson Library Bulletin*, 327.

29. Jack Forman, letter, *Wilson Library Bulletin*, December 1981, 246.

30. Mel Rosenberg, letter, *Wilson Library Bulletin*, December 1981, 246.

31. Pelorus, *Signal*, 146.

32. Grove, "Robert Cormier Comes of Age," 78.

33. Schwartz, "Teen-agers' Laureate," 88.

34. Grove, "Robert Cormier Comes of Age," 82.

35. Davis, "Tough Tales," 33.

36. Graeber, "Robert Cormier," 98.

37. De Luca and Natov, "Interview with Robert Cormier," 114.

38. Robert Cormier, letter to eighth grade students at Eli and Bessie Cohen Hillel Academy, Swampscott, Massachusetts, 13 November 1982. Robert E. Cormier Collection, Fitchburg State College, Fitchburg, Massachusetts.

39. De Luca and Natov, "Interview with Robert Cormier," 120.

40. Ibid., 114.

41. Cormier, "Forever Pedaling."

42. Schwartz, "Teen-agers' Laureate," 88.

43. De Luca and Natov, "Interview with Robert Cormier," 118.

Chapter 6

1. Anita Silvey, "An Interview with Robert Cormier," *Horn Book*, part 1, March/April 1985, 145; part 2, May/June 1985, 289.
2. Silvey interview, *Horn Book*, part 2, 289.
3. Silvey interview, *Horn Book*, part 1, 145.
4. Ibid.
5. Ibid.
6. Ibid.
7. Ibid.
8. Ibid.
9. Silvey interview, *Horn Book*, part 2, 289.
10. Silvey interview, *Horn Book*, part 1, 145.
11. Roger Sutton, review of *Beyond the Chocolate War, School Library Journal*, April 1985, 96.
12. Hazel Rochman, review of *Beyond the Chocolate War, New York Times Book Review*, 5 May 1985, 37.
13. Sally Estes, review of *Beyond the Chocolate War, Booklist*, 15 March 1985, 1048.
14. Marcia Cohen, review of *Beyond the Chocolate War, Seventeen*, August 1985, 184.
15. Stephanie Nettell, "Paperbacks in Brief," [London] *Times Literary Supplement*, 3 April 1987, 358.
16. Mary M. Burns, review of *Beyond the Chocolate War, Horn Book*, July/August 1985, 451.
17. Gayle Keresey, review of *Beyond the Chocolate War, Voice of Youth Advocates*, June 1985, 128.
18. Burns review, *Horn Book*, 451.

Chapter 7

1. Newgate Callender, "Boy on the Couch," *New York Times Book Review*, 1 May 1977, 26.
2. Perry Nodelman, "Robert Cormier Does a Number," *Children's Literature in Education*, Summer 1983, 94.
3. De Luca and Natov, "Interview with Robert Cormier," 128.
4. Nodelman, "Number," 96–97.
5. De Luca and Natov, "Interview with Robert Cormier," 129.
6. Nilsen, "The Poetry of Naming," 3.
7. De Luca and Natov, "Interview with Robert Cormier," 128.
8. Robert Cormier, answer sheet for readers' questions on *I Am the Cheese*, Robert E. Cormier Collection, Fitchburg State College, Fitchburg, Massachusetts.

9. MacLeod, "Robert Cormier and the Adolescent Novel," 77.
10. Ibid., 76.
11. Bruce Clements, review of *I Am the Cheese, Horn Book*, August 1977, 427.
12. Lance Salway, review of *I Am the Cheese*, [London] *Times Literary Supplement*, 2 December 1977, 1415.
13. Review of *I Am the Cheese, Publishers Weekly*, 7 March 1977, 100.
14. Review of *I Am the Cheese, West Coast Review of Books*, September 1977, 55.
15. Callendar, "Boy on the Couch," 26.
16. Cormier, "The Cheerful Side of Controversy," 6.
17. De Luca and Natov, "Interview with Robert Cormier," 123.
18. McLaughlin, *Cheese, Chocolates, and Kids*.
19. De Luca and Natov, "Interview with Robert Cormier," 124.
20. Robert Cormier, letter to author, 25 January 1984.
21. De Luca and Natov, "Interview with Robert Cormier," 127.
22. "Robert Cormier: His Novels Focus on the Teenage Years," *Read Magazine*, 20 May 1983.

Chapter 8

1. Grove, "Robert Cormier Comes of Age," 79.
2. De Luca and Natov, "Interview with Robert Cormier," 132.
3. Cormier, speech at YASD luncheon.
4. De Luca and Natov, "Interview with Robert Cormier," 130.
5. Nilsen, "The Poetry of Naming," 3.
6. Ibid.
7. Lenz, "A Romantic Ironist's Vision."
8. Barbara Harrison, *Horn Book*, August 1979, 426.
9. De Luca and Natov, "Interview with Robert Cormier," 132.
10. MacLeod, "Robert Cormier and the Adolescent Novel," 77–78.
11. Cormier, " 'Are You Working on a New Novel?,' " 1.
12. *Publishers Weekly*, 7 March 1977, 100.
13. "Soldiers at Ft. Bragg Debate Lost Mission," *Los Angeles Times*, 27 April 1980, 16.

Chapter 9

1. Cormier, *Eight Plus One*, jacket flap.
2. E. L. Heins, review of *Eight Plus One, Horn Book*, October 1980, 524.

3. R. Wilson, review of *Eight Plus One, Washington Post Book World*, 11 January 1981, 7.

4. Review of *Eight Plus One, Kirkus Reviews*, 15 November 1980, 1469.

5. Benjamin De Mott, review of *Eight Plus One, New York Times*, 9 November 1980, 55.

6. Cyrisse Jaffee, review of *Eight Plus One, School Library Journal*, September 1980, 81.

7. John Dinolfo, "Exclusive: An Interview with Robert Cormier," *You and Your World*, Teacher's Edition, part 1, 3 December 1980, 1.

8. Review of *Take Me Where the Good Times Are, Kirkus Reviews*, 1 February 1965, 132.

9. Harold C. Gardiner, review of *Take Me Where the Good Times Are, America*, 15 May 1965, 717.

10. William B. Hill, review of *A Little Raw on Monday Mornings, Best Sellers*, 1 October 1963, 222.

11. Genevieve M. Casey, review of *A Little Raw on Monday Mornings, Library Journal*, 1 September 1963, 3101.

12. Cormier, *Eight Plus One*, 78–79.

13. Phoebe-Lou Adams, review of *Now and at the Hour, Atlantic*, September 1960, 118.

14. Riley Hughes, review of *Now and at the Hour, Catholic Library World*, December 1960, 182.

15. Mary Ross, review of *Now and at the Hour, Herald Tribune Book Review*, 31 July 1960, 4.

Chapter 10

1. Graeber, "PW Interviews," 98.

2. Hazel Rochman, review of *The Bumblebee Flies Anyway, School Library Journal*, September 1983, 132.

3. Sally Estes, review of *The Bumblebee Flies Anyway, Booklist*, 1 September 1983, 37.

4. Thomas M. Disch, "Boys on the Brink," *Washington Post Book World*, 6 November 1983.

5. Ernest Hemingway, *Death in the Afternoon* (New York: Charles Scribner's Sons, 1932), 122.

Chapter 11

1. Robert Cormier, "Creating *Fade*," *Horn Book*, March/April 1989, 166.

2. Stephen King, letter to editors of Delacorte Press, 10 May 1987.
3. James Hastings, ed., *Encyclopedia of Religion and Ethics* (New York: Charles Scribner's Sons, 1955), 406.
4. H. G. Wells, *The Invisible Man*. In *Seven Science Fiction Novels of H. G. Wells* (New York: Dover, 1934).
5. Thomas Berger, *Being Invisible* (Boston: Little, Brown, 1987).
6. H. F. Saint, *Memoirs of an Invisible Man* (New York: Atheneum, 1987).
7. Berger, *Being Invisible*, 41.
8. Wells, *The Invisible Man*, 268.
9. Pauline Kael, *5001 Nights at the Movies* (New York: Holt, Rinehart & Winston, 1984), 282.
10. Robert Cormier, "A Boy Who Possesses Animal Magnetism," *Los Angeles Times*, 6 December 1986, part 5, 14.
11. Cormier, "Creating *Fade*," 166.
12. King, letter to Delacorte Press.
13. Cormier, "Creating *Fade*," 166.
14. Ibid.
15. R. D., "A Look at the Creative Process," *Publishers Weekly*, 29 July 1988, 134.
16. Zena Sutherland, *Bulletin of the Center for Children's Books*, November 1988, 68.
17. Cormier, "Creating *Fade*," 166.
18. Sutherland, *Bulletin of the Center for Children's Books*, 68.
19. *Kirkus Reviews*, 1 August 1988, 1147.
20. Hazel Rochman, *Booklist*, 1 September 1988, 67.
21. Cathi MacRae, *Wilson Library Bulletin*, February 1989, 86.
22. Beverly Lyon Clark, *New York Times Book Review*, 12 February 1989, 18.
23. Anita Silvey, *Horn Book*, March/April 1985, 145.

Appendix

1. Courtemanche, "Robert Cormier—in the Movies," 8.
2. Ibid., 9.
3. Rex Reed, *New York Post*, 11 November 1983, 14.
4. Press kit for *The Chocolate War*, Management Company Entertainment Group.
5. Robert Cormier, letter to author, 11 June 1984.
6. Interview with Keith Gordon, 13 September 1988.
7. Ibid.
8. Press kit, MCEG.
9. Jack Lechner, "The Chocolate War," *American Film*, November 1988, 9.

Selected Bibliography

Primary Works

Novels

After the First Death. New York: Pantheon Books, 1979; Avon, 1980.
Beyond the Chocolate War. New York: Pantheon Books, 1985.
The Bumblebee Flies Anyway. New York: Pantheon Books, 1983; Dell, 1984.
The Chocolate War. New York: Pantheon Books, 1974; Dell, 1975; Listening Library, 1988 (audiocassete).
Fade. New York: Delacorte, 1988.
I Am the Cheese. New York: Pantheon Books, 1977; Dell, 1978.
A Little Raw on Monday Mornings. New York: Sheed & Ward, 1963; Avon, 1980.
Now and at the Hour. New York: Coward-McCann, 1960; Avon, 1980.
Take Me Where the Good Times Are. New York: Macmillan, 1965; Avon, 1981.

Unpublished Novels

"Act of Contrition" (first and second version).
"In the Midst of Winter."
"The Rumple Country."

Short Stories

"And All Our Yesterdays. . . ." *Savior's Call*, February 1945, 2.
"Anniversary." *Sign*, September 1954, 2.
"Anniversary." *Toronto Star Weekly*, 8 June 1955.
"Another of Mike's Girls." *McCalls*, November 1973, 2.

"A Bad Time for Fathers." *Woman's Day*, October 1970, 1.
"A Bad Time for Fathers." *Woman's Own*, 3 July 1971.
"Between the Darkness and the Daylight." *Sign*, January 1968, 6.
"Bunny Berigan—Wasn't He a Musician or Something?" *Redbook*, January 1966, 3.
"Bunny Berigan—Wasn't He a Musican or Something?" *Woman's Mirror*, January 1967.
"The Busted Heart." *Sign*, April 1951.
"Charlie Mitchell, You Rat, Be Kind to My Little Girl." *McCalls*, April 1969, 7.
"Color Scheme." *Sign*, September 1947, 2.
"The Crush." *Sign*, August 1966, 1.
"The Day of Fire Engines." *St. Anthony's Messenger*, January 1971, 8.
Eight Plus One: Stories. New York: Pantheon Books, 1980; Bantam, 1982.
"An Elegy for Edgar." *Sign*, January 1949, 6.
"Eye of the Beholder." *Sign*, March 1957, 8.
"First Chance." *Sign*, January 1957, 6.
"The First Day." *Sign*, November 1953, 4.
"The Flutter as of Wings." *Sign*, December 1955, 5.
"Full Count." *Sign*, July 1957, 11.
"The Gesture." *Sign*, January 1952, 16.
"The Gift." *Sign*, November 1949, 4.
"Goodbye, Little Girl." *Woman's Own*, 5 July 1969.
"Guess What? I Almost Kissed My Father Goodnight." *Saturday Evening Post*, Winter 1971, 3.
"The Heart of Mrs. Bonville." *Sign*, December 1952, 5.
"In the Heat." In *Sixteen*. New York: Delacorte, 1984; Listening Library, 1987 (audiocassette).
"Let's Try for a Happy Ending Anyway." *St. Anthony's Messenger*, September 1967, 4.
"The Little Things That Count." *Sign*, May 1944, 1.
"The May Basket." *Sign*, December 1947, 10.
"The Mill." *Sign*, May 1954, 10.
"Mine on Thursdays." *Woman's Day*, October 1968, 1.
"A Moment of Wisdom." *New York Telegram*, 16 April 1955.
"The Moustache." *Scholastic Voice*, 31 October 1980.
"The Moustache." *Woman's Day*, November 1975.
"My Father's Gamble." *Sign*, April 1961.
"My First Negro." *Sign*, March 1969, 8.
"No Time to Be Far from Embraces." *Extension*, November 1967, 6.
"The Other Side of the Mountain." *Sign*, January 1954, 6.
"President Cleveland, Where Are You?" *Redbook*, May 1965, 1.

"Pretend, A Verb: To Make Believe. . . ." *St. Anthony's Messenger*, April 1967, 11.
"Protestants Cry Too." *St. Anthony's Messenger*, January 1967, 8.
"The Soldier." *Sign*, July 1945, 12.
"Spoiled Girl." *Sign*, June 1958, 11.
"Spring Will Come Again." *Sign*, March 1946, 8.
"The Tenderness." *Sign*, December 1947, 5.
"Uncle Jay's Last Christmas." *Sign*, December 1949, 5.

Nonfiction

And So On—: The John Fitch IV Columns by Robert Cormier. Edited with an introduction by Constance Senay Cormier. New York: Delacorte, forthcoming.
Articles. *Fitchburg Sentinel-Enterprise*, 1955–78.
"Books Remembered." *The Calendar*, Children's Book Council, June/December 1986, unpaginated.
"A Boy Who Possesses Animal Magnetism." Review of *The Flight of the Cassowary* by John LeVert. *Los Angeles Times*, 6 December 1986, part 5, 14.
"The Citizens of Cormier County." Pamphlet. New York: Dell, 1988.
Columns. [John Fitch IV, pseud.] *Fitchburg Sentinel-Enterprise*, 1966–78.
"Creating *Fade*." *Horn Book*, March/April 1989, 166.
"Forever Pedaling on the Road to Realism." In *Celebrating Children's Books: Essays on Children's Literature in Honor of Zena Sutherland*, edited by Betsy Hearne and Marilyn Kaye. New York: Lothrop, Lee & Shepard, 1981.
"Robert Cormier." Pamphlet. New York: Pantheon Books, Library Marketing, n.d.

Speeches

Speech at Young Adult Services Division luncheon, American Library Association Conference, Dallas, Texas, June 1979. Audiocassette.
"The Cormier Novels: The Cheerful Side of Controversy." Speech given at the Cervantes Convention and Exhibit Center [n.p.]; sponsored by the Children's Libraries Section of the Catholic Library Association, 29 March 1978. *Catholic Library World*, July 1978, 6.

Secondary Works

Books, Pamphlets, and Parts of Books

Commire, Anne, ed. *Something about the Author*. Detroit: Gale, 1976, 10:28.

Contemporary Literary Criticism. Detroit: Gale, 1973, 133.

Donelson, Kenneth L., and Alleen Pace Nilsen. *Literature for Today's Young Adults*. Glenview, Ill.: Scott, Foresman & Co., 1980.

Lesniak, James G. "Robert Cormier." In *Contemporary Authors*, New Revision Series. Detroit: Gale, 1981, 5:130.

Sarkissian, Adele, ed. *Children's Authors and Illustrators: An Index to Biographical Dictionaries*. 2d ed. Detroit: Gale, 1978.

Stanek, Lou Willett. A *Study Guide to "After the First Death" by Robert Cormier*. New York: Avon, n.d.

———. *A Teacher's Guide to the Paperback Edition of "The Chocolate War" by Robert Cormier*. New York: Dell, 1975.

———. *A Teacher's Guide to the Paperback Edition of "I Am the Cheese" by Robert Cormier*. New York: Dell, 1978.

Stines, Joe. "Robert Cormier." In *Dictionary of Literary Biography. American Writers for Children Since 1960: Fiction*. Detroit: Gale, 1986, 52:107.

Articles

Bagnall, Norma. "Realism: How Realistic Is It: A Look at *The Chocolate War*." *Top of the News*, Winter 1980, 214.

Carter, Betty, and Karen Harris. "Realism in Adolescent Fiction: In Defense of *The Chocolate War*." *Top of the News*, Winter, 1980, 283.

Clements, Bruce. "A Second Look: *The Chocolate War*." *Horn Book*, April 1979, 217.

Courtemanche, Dolores. "Overnight Success—after 30 Years." *Worcester Sunday Telegram*, 18 July 1982, 11.

———. "Robert Cormier—in the Movies." *Worcester Sunday Telegram*, 18 July 1982, 8.

Daly, Jay. "The New Repression." *Top of the News*, Fall 1980, 79.

Davis, William A. "Tough Tales for Teenagers." *Boston Globe Magazine*, 16 November 1980, 17.

Dudar, Helen. "What Johnny Can't Read." *Soho News*, 4 June 1980, 12.

Gallo, Donald R. "Reality and Responsibility: The Continuing Controversy over Robert Cormier's Books for Young Adults." *Voice of Youth Advocates*, December 1984, 245.

Gottlieb, Annie. "A New Cycle in YA Books." *New York Times Book Review*, 17 June 1984, 24.
Grove, Lee. "Robert Cormier Comes of Age." *Boston Magazine*, December 1980, 78.
Knudsen, Elizabeth G. "Is There Hope for Young Adult Readers?" *Wilson Library Bulletin*, September 1981, 47.
Loer, Stephanie. "Leominster's Inventive Son." *Boston Globe,* 30 January 1989, 9.
Lukens, Rebecca. "From Salinger to Cormier: Disillusionment to *Despair in Thirty Years*." ALAN Review, Fall 1981, 38.
MacLeod, Anne Scott. "Robert Cormier and the Adolescent Novel." *Children's Literature in Education*, Summer 1981, 76.
Nilsen, Alleen Pace. "The Poetry of Naming in Young Adult Books." *ALAN Review*, Spring 1980, 3.
Nodelman, Perry. "Robert Cormier Does a Number." *Children's Literature in Education*, Summer 1983, 94.
Schwartz, Tony. "Teen-agers' Laureate." *Newsweek*, 16 July 1979, 87.
Stoddart, Patricia, and Joyce Kinkead. "Pen-Pals and *I Am the Cheese*." *ALAN Review*, Fall 1987, 40.
Sutton, Roger. "The Critical Myth: Realistic YA Novels." *School Library Journal*, November 1982, 33.

Published Letters

Bronson, Diane. *Wilson Library Bulletin*, December 1981, 247.
Duter, Judith A. *Newsweek*, 13 August 1979, 6.
Fabian, William. *Wilson Library Bulletin*, November 1981, 167.
Forman, Jack. *Wilson Library Bulletin*, December 1981, 246.
Hoxie, Renee. *Wilson Library Bulletin*, January 1982, 327.
McCarrell, Sharon. *Wilson Library Bulletin*, November 1981, 167.
Rosenberg, Mel. *Wilson Library Bulletin*, December 1981, 246.
Rosenfeld, Judith. *School Library Journal*, September 1980, 3.
Thomas, Sharon. *Wilson Library Bulletin*, December 1981, 246.
Thompson, Paulette. *Newsweek*, 13 August 1979, 6.

Interviews

Christian, George. "Conversations: Novelist Robert Cormier and Reporter Nora Ephron." *Houston Chronicle*, 14 May 1978, 12.
"Close-up: Robert Cormier, Novelist." *Fiction Writer's Market*, May 1983, 500.

Cormier, Robert. " 'Are You Working on a New Novel?' 'Yes.' " *ALAN Review*, Winter 1980, 1.
De Luca, Geraldine, and Natov, Roni. "An Interview with Robert Cormier." *Lion and the Unicorn*, Fall 1978, 109.
Dinolfo, John. "Exclusive: An Interview with Robert Cormier." *You and Your World*, Teacher's Edition. Part 1, 3 December 1980; part 2, 10 December 1980.
Graeber, Laurel. "PW Interviews: Robert Cormier." *Publishers Weekly*, 7 October 1983, 98.
Irwin, Victoria. "I Enjoy Writing About Young People Because I Feel an Affinity for Them." *Christian Science Monitor*, 20 May 1980, 23.
Janeczco, Paul. "An Interview with Robert Cormier." *English Journal*, September 1977, 10.
McLaughlin, Frank. *Cheese, Chocolates, and Kids: A Day with Robert Cormier*. Videotape prepared for PBS, n.d. Robert E. Cormier Collection, Fitchburg State College, Fitchburg, Massachusetts.
———. "Robert Cormier: A Profile." *Media and Methods*, May/June 1978, 28.
"Robert Cormier: His Novels Focus on the Teenage Years." *Read Magazine*, 20 May 1983.
Rosenberg, Merri. "Teenagers Face Evil." *New York Times Book Review*, 5 May 1985, 36.
Silvey, Anita. "An Interview with Robert Cormier." *Horn Book*, part 1, March/April 1985, 145; part 2, May/June 1985, 289.

Speeches

Gallo, Donald R. "Robert Cormier: The Author and the Man." Speech at a reception commemorating the establishment of the Robert Cormier Collection, Fitchburg State College Library, Fitchburg, Massachusetts, 3 May 1981. *ALAN Review*, Fall 1981, 34.
Lenz, Millicent. "A Romantic Ironist's Vision of Evil: Robert Cormier's *After the First Death*." Paper presented at the Eighth Annual Conference of the Children's Literature Association, Minneapolis, Minnesota, March 1981.

Selected Book Reviews

After the First Death

Booklist, 15 March 1979, 1141.
Bulletin of the Center for Children's Books, June 1979, 172.
Campbell, Patty. *Wilson Library Bulletin*, April 1979, 578.

Davis, L. J. *Washington Post Book World*, 13 May 1979, K3.
Ellin, Stanley. "You Can and Can't Go Home Again." *New York Times Book Review*, 29 April 1979, 30.
Harrison, Barbara. *Horn Book*, August 1979, 426.
Hibberd, Dominic. "Missing the Bus." [London] *Times Literary Supplement*, 14 December 1979, 125.
Hirsch, Lorraine. *Christian Science Monitor*, 1 June 1979, 22.
Kirkus Reviews, 1 April 1979, 391.
Norsworthy, James A. *Catholic Library World*, November 1979, 182.
Pollack, Pamela. *School Library Journal*, March 1979, 146.
Publishers Weekly, 29 January 1979, 115.

Beyond the Chocolate War

Bulletin of the Center for Children's Books, April 1985, 143.
Burns, Mary M. *Horn Book*, July/August 1985, 451.
Cohen, Marcia. *Seventeen*, August 1985, 184.
Estes, Sally. *Booklist*, 15 March 1985, 1048.
Hayes, Sarah. "One Black Marble." [London] *Times Literary Supplement*, 29 November 1985, 1358.
Keresey, Gayle. *Voice of Youth Advocates*, June 1985, 128.
Kirkus Reviews, 1 March 1985, J17.
Nelms, Beth, Ben Nelms, and Linda Horton. *English Journal*, September 1985, 85.
Nettell, Stephanie. "Paperbacks in Brief." [London] *Times Literary Supplement*, 3 April 1987, 358.
Publishers Weekly, 15 February 1985, 102.
Rochman, Hazel. *New York Times Book Review*, 5 May 1985, 37.
Silvey, Anita. "An Interview with Robert Cormier." *Horn Book*, part 1, March/April 1985, 145; part 2, May/June 1985, 289.
Sutton, Roger. *School Library Journal*, April 1985, 96.

The Bumblebee Flies Anyway

Abrahamson, Dick, Betty Carter, and Barbara Samuels. "A Bountiful Harvest of Young Adult Books." *English Journal*, October 1983, 84.
Basbanes, Nicholas. "Cormier Launches *Bumblebee*." *Worcester Evening Gazette*, 14 September 1983, 3.
Bulletin of the Center for Children's Books, September 1983, 3.
Cooper, Ilene. *Booklist*, 1 September 1983, 82.
Disch, Thomas M. "Boys on the Brink." *Washington Post Book World*, 6 November 1983.
Ellis, W. Geiger, *ALAN Review*, Fall 1983, 23.
Estes, Sally. *Booklist*, 1 September 1983, 37.
Horowitz, Anthony. [London] *Times Literary Supplement*, 25 November 1983, 1318.

Kirkus Reviews, 1 September 1983, J-172.
Knowles, John. "Defiance and Survival." *New York Times*, 13 November 1983.
Loescher, Judy. "Cormier's *Bumblebee* Stings." *Fitchburg Sentinel-Enterprise*, 8 September 1983, 20.
Madden, Susan B. *Voice of Youth Advocates*, December 1983, 278.
N.C.H. *Horn Book*, December 1983, 715.
Publishers Weekly, 5 August 1983, 92.
Rochman, Hazel. *School Library Journal*, September 1983, 132.

The Chocolate War

Bulletin of the Center for Children's Books, July 1974, 173.
Chelton, Mary K. *School Library Journal*, May 1974, 62.
Fagg, Martin. "Beasts and Monks." *New Statesman*, 23 May 1975, 694.
Fisher, Margery. *Growing Point*, July 1975, 2656.
Hearne, Betsy. "Whammo, You Lose." *Booklist*, July 1974, 1199.
Hunt, Peter. [London] *Times Literary Supplement*, 4 April 1975, 364.
Junior Bookshelf, June 1975, 194.
Kirkus Reviews, 1 April 1974, 371.
Peck, Richard. "Delivering the Goods." *American Libraries*, October 1974, 492.
Pelorus. *Signal*, September 1975, 146.
Publishers Weekly, 15 April 1974, 52.
Weesner, Theodore. *New York Times*, 5 May 1974, 15.

Eight Plus One

Bulletin of the Center for Children's Books, December 1980, 67.
De Mott, Benjamin. *New York Times*, 9 November 1980, 55.
Heins, P. L. *Horn Book*, October 1980, 524.
Jaffee, Cyrisse. *School Library Journal*, September 1980, 81.
Kirkus Reviews, 15 November 1980, 1469.
Lenz, Millicent. *Voice of Youth Advocates*, December 1980, 28.
Publishers Weekly, 29 August 1980, 365.
Wilson, R. *Washington Post Book World*, 11 January 1981, 7.
Zvirin, Stephanie. *Booklist*, 15 September 1980, 110.

Fade

Clark, Beverly Lyon. *New York Times Book Review*, 12 February 1989, 18.
Fakih, Kimberly Olson, and Diane Roback. *Publishers Weekly*, 30 September 1988, 69.
Kirkus Reviews, 1 August 1988, 1147.
MacRae, Cathi. *Wilson Library Bulletin*, February 1989, 86.
Pickworth, Hannah. *ALAN Review*, Fall 1988, 19.

R. D. "A Look at the Creative Process." *Publishers Weekly*, 29 July 1988, 134.

Rochman, Hazel. *Booklist*, 1 September 1988, 67.

Sutherland, Zena. *Bulletin of the Center for Children's Books*, November 1988, 68.

Unsworth, Robert. *School Library Journal*, October 1988, 160.

I Am the Cheese

Bell, Robert. *School Librarian*, September 1978, 281.

Booklist, 1 April 1977, 1155.

Bulletin of the Center for Children's Books, April 1977, 121.

Callendar, Newgate. "Boy on the Couch." *New York Times Book Review*, 1 May 1977, 26.

Heins, Paul. *Horn Book*, August 1977, 427.

Junior Bookshelf, June 1978, 150.

Kirkus Reviews, 1 March 1977, 237.

May, Clifford D. "Catchers in the Rye." *Newsweek*, 19 December 1977, 85.

Norsworthy, James A. *Catholic Library World*, December 1977, 234.

Publishers Weekly, 7 March 1977, 100.

Salway, Lance. [London] *Times Literary Supplement*, 2 December 1977, 1415.

School Library Journal, May 1977, 78.

A Little Raw on Monday Mornings

Casey, Genevieve M. *Library Journal*, 1 September 1963, 3101.

Christian Century, 25 September 1963, 1171.

Hill, William B. *Best Sellers*, 1 October 1963, 222.

Now and at the Hour

Adams, Phoebe-Lou. *Atlantic*, September 1960, 118.

Fitchburg Sentinel-Enterprise, 2 August 1960, 6.

Hughes, Riley. *Catholic Library World*, December 1960, 182.

Serebnick, Judith. "Triumph in Tragedy." *Library Journal*, 1 June 1960, 2203.

Time, 1 August 1960, 68.

Take Me Where the Good Times Are

Gardiner, Harold C. *America*, 15 May 1965, 717.

Henderson, Robert W. *Library Journal*, 15 March 1965, 1345.

Levin, Martin. *New York Times Book Review*, 25 April 1965, 425.

Murray, Michele. *Commonweal*, 2 July 1965, 477.

Index

Key:
After the First Death = AFD
Beyond the Chocolate War = BCW
The Bumblebee Flies Anyway = BB
The Chocolate War = CW
Fade = F
I Am the Cheese = IAC
A Little Raw on Monday Mornings = LR
Now and at the Hour = NaaH
Take Me Where the Good Times Are = TMW

About the Author

Patricia J. Campbell is general editor of the Twayne Young Adult Author Series and an author, critic, and former librarian. Among her other books are *Sex Guides* and *Passing the Hat: Street Performers in America*. She writes a monthly column about unusual books for the Wilson Library Bulletin and for ten years wrote "The YA Perplex" for that journal. She has taught adolescent literature at UCLA Extension and reviews sporadically for the *New York Times* and other publications. Campbell and her husband, David Shore, together research and write books about camper-van travel in exotic locations.